In Search of History

History

1714–1900

J.F. Aylett

Hodder & Stoughton

A MEMBER OF THE HODDER HEADLINE GROUP

For my aunts

The solutions to the two detective cases on page 41 may be found in *The First Detectives* by Belton Cobb (Faber and Faber, 1957), along with details of many other early cases.

The letter from Ned Ludd on page 45 has been transcribed from the original.

Illustrations by Philip Page

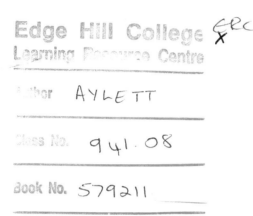

British Library Cataloguing in Publication Data
Aylett, J. F.
    In search of history: 1714–1900.
    1. Great Britain——Social conditions——18th
century——2. Great Britain——Social conditions——19th
century
    I. Title
    941.07   HN385

    ISBN 0 7131 0687 5

First published 1985
Impression number   15 14 13
Year   1999 1998 1997 1996

Printed in Great Britain for Hodder & Stoughton Educational, a division of Hodder Headline Plc, 338 Euston Road, London NW1 3BH by The Bath Press, Bath

Acknowledgements

Evidence D on page 47 is from *The Blockers' Seaside* by C J Peaple and appears by permission of the author. Every effort has been made to trace any other possible copyright holders but, in a few cases, this has not been possible. The publishers will be pleased to make good any omissions in future editions of the book.

The Publishers wish to thank the following for their permission to reproduce copyright illustrations:

Crown copyright, Science Museum, London: p 89; Rothamsted Experimental Station: p 7; Gloucester Record Office: p 9; BBC Hulton Picture Library: pp 11, 21b, 25, 66, 75l, 80r, 84r; Bolton Museums & Art Gallery: p 13; Mansell Collection: pp 14, 15, 17tl & tr & bl, 18cr, 31r, 32, 33, 37, 44, 47t & b, 48t, 49t, 53, 61, 68, 72, 74r, 77, 83, 84l; Mary Evans Picture Library: pp 18tl, 22, 67; British Library: pp 18bl, 19r, 49c (text); National Museum of Labour History: pp 19l, 75r; New Lanark Conservation Trust: p 60; taken from *The Industrial Revolution 1760–1860* by Beggs Humphreys: p 21tr; Museum of London: pp 23, 87b; Illustrated London News: pp 27, 57, 69b, 74l; CH Wood-500 Video, Bradford: p 30; Wellcome Institute Library, London: pp 31l, 73t & b, 80l; British Museum: p 34; T & R Annan & Sons, Glasgow: p 35t; Guildhall Library: p 35b, 65b; Cambridgeshire Police Historical Society: p 39; Chief Constable, Essex Police: p 40; Metropolitan Police: p 41; Kingston upon Hull Museums & Art Galleries: pp 42, 43t; Trustees of the Wedgewood Museum, Barlaston, Staffs: p 43b; taken from *Captain Swing* by Hobsbawn & Rudé: p 46; Hall & Woodhouse Ltd: p 48b; *Punch*: pp 51, 65t, 69t, 82; National Railway Museum, York: pp 54, 55; Leicester Museum: p 59; British Newspaper Library (BL): pp 49b, 70, 71l; taken from *An Economic & Social History of Britain since 1700* by M W Flinn: p 71r; National Gallery of Art, Washington (Rosenwald Collection): p 76; taken from *A Course Book in British Social & Economic History from 1760* by P F Speed: p 79; J Sainsbury plc: p 85; Stanley Gibbons Ltd: p 86bl; Telecom Technology Showcase: p 87t; Science Museum: p 90; Caliban Books: p 94l; taken from *Human Documents of the Industrial Revolution in Britain* by E Royston Pike: p 94r.

The author wishes to thank the Greater Manchester Museum of Science and Industry for providing information for this book.

Contents

Introduction

Today, I am writing this book. How do I know? Because I am here. I am doing it.

Last week, some men began building some new houses near where I live. How do I know? Because I was here when it happened. I watched them lifting the roof into position.

In the late 19th century, my grandfather left school. He was about 12 years old and his first job was on a farm. He had to scare the birds away from the crops – for 25p a week. How do I know? Because, years ago, he told me about it. It was something he had done.

In 1837, Victoria became Queen of England. How do I know? I wasn't there. I can't remember it. I have certainly never met anyone who was there. It was too long ago. So how do I know?

I expect I read about it in a book. But how did the writer know? Many writers wrote about events they did not witness.

The writers must have had a reason for writing it. They must have had some *evidence* to make them believe it. How *do* people know what happened in 1837?

This is how we know:

Some people wrote about it at the time.

Some people told their friends . . . and they told their friends . . . and, later on, somebody wrote about it.

Some people made pictures of it. A few decades later, people were taking photographs of big events. And, by the end of the century, there were even people making films.

And some people left behind things which we can still look at today.

So we ought to know what happened. The trouble is that people do not always agree about what happened. Sometimes, writers are biased; sometimes, they forget; and, sometimes, they make mistakes and get things wrong. So we must be careful when we read or look at primary sources.

In any case, history is more than just finding out what happened. Historians also want to know *why* things happened. Look at the graph below.

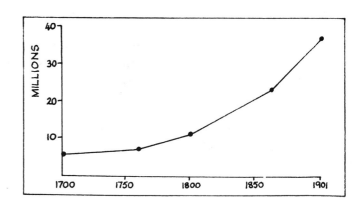

PRIMARY AND SECONDARY SOURCES

The historian makes use of two kinds of sources. Primary sources were made or written at the time the events happened. Secondary sources are written or produced after the event, by someone who was not there. Nearly all the pictures and extracts used in the evidence sections of this book are primary sources.

In just over 100 years after 1688, the population doubled. Then, in the next 50 years, it doubled again. We know it happened. But why did it happen?

Now, look at the map on the right. Where did most people live in 1701? When you have worked that out, look at the second map. What changes had taken place by 1801?

One main change was that more people lived in towns in 1801 than in 1701. Some of these towns were very big and quite new. Why did they suddenly grow up? What had happened?

There are many answers to these questions. But one is simple and straightforward. Britain had been going through huge changes in industry and farming. A whole range of new machines had been invented; all sorts of new ideas were being tried out.

Of course, history is the story of what *people* have done in the past. People are more important than machines. This book is mostly about people and how they lived in the 18th and 19th centuries. But we can not ignore the machines. Sooner or later, they affected nearly everyone's lives.

So this book begins by looking at some of these new ideas and machines. And we start with farming. . . .

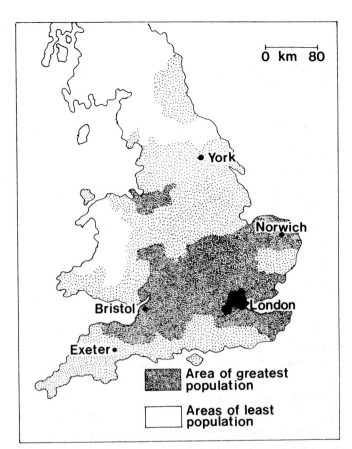

Above: map showing where people lived in 1701. Below: where people lived in 1801. (The towns marked were the largest at those times.)

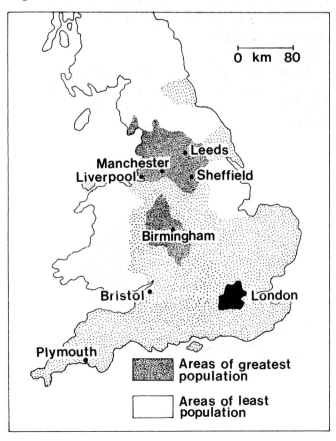

5

1 Changes on the Farms

Seed had always been sown by hand. This is called broadcasting. The numbers give clues about how seed was wasted. (See question 2.)

Every human being needs food. Without food, we would die. It is so obvious that you hardly ever see it written down. The **population** of Britain grew rapidly in the 18th century. So there had to be more food. And the farmers had to grow it.

They used new methods and new machines to help them. These changes were so great that historians talk about a revolution in agriculture – the Agricultural Revolution.

A few men led the way in this revolution and thousands more followed. One of the leaders was Jethro Tull, a farmer from Berkshire. He invented two machines.

One was a seed drill which sowed seeds in straight lines. The results were bigger crops and less seed wasted. The other was a hoe pulled by a horse, for weeding between rows of growing crops. It was quicker than doing it by hand.

He wrote about his ideas in a book called *Horse-hoeing Husbandry* in 1731. But people did not pay him much attention at the time because he got so many other things wrong. He said that farmers should not manure their crops, but other farmers knew they should. Even his own farm workers thought he was a crank.

Jethro Tull's seed drill.

Meanwhile, in Norfolk, other farmers copied ideas which had been used in Holland. One of these farmers was Lord Townshend. People nicknamed him 'Turnip' because he believed in growing turnips as winter food for cattle. It was not a new idea but he was so well-known that he helped to make it popular.

Growing turnips became part of a whole new system of farming. We call it the Norfolk Rotation. It involved growing four different crops over four years in each field. That way, the field was never left fallow (unused), as it had been in the past. The diagram below shows why.

1ST YEAR

WHEAT (for bread)

2ND YEAR

TURNIPS (cattle food) THEY CLEANSED THE SOIL

3RD YEAR

BARLEY (for beer)

4TH YEAR

GRASSES. (Clover takes nitrogen from the air. When dug in, this makes soil richer.)

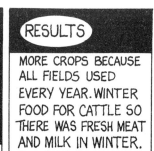

RESULTS

MORE CROPS BECAUSE ALL FIELDS USED EVERY YEAR. WINTER FOOD FOR CATTLE SO THERE WAS FRESH MEAT AND MILK IN WINTER. SCURVY BECAME LESS COMMON.

While some farmers were growing more crops, others were producing more meat. Robert Bakewell led the way. He produced bigger sheep on his Leicestershire farm. In the past, sheep had been bred mainly for wool. Bakewell bred big, fat sheep to eat.

He was less successful when it came to breeding better cattle. But his ideas were used by Charles and Robert Colling from Durham. They produced better cattle called Durham Shorthorns. Other people were soon using the ideas to produce bigger pigs and better horses.

They were not the only ones with ideas. Thomas Coke (you say it: cook) improved the sandy soil on his Norfolk estate by a method called **marling**. He also held a sheep-shearing festival every year. People even turned up from America to learn about his methods.

King George III also spread ideas by writing about farming and he set up a model farm on his estate at Windsor. People actually called him 'Farmer George'.

1 Match up the names on the left with the correct description from the right:

Jethro Tull	improved sheep
Robert Bakewell	held sheep–shearing events
Colling Brothers	invented a seed drill
Lord Townshend	improved shorthorn cattle
Thomas Coke	famous for growing turnips

2 a) List the ways in which broadcast sowing wasted seeds.
   b) Draw Tull's seed drill.
   c) Why was it better than broadcast sowing?
3 a) Copy the diagram of the Norfolk Rotation.
   b) What other results could you add to box 5?
   c) Why was this system better for (i) farmers and (ii) the British people?
4 a) Copy down the figures in evidence B.
   b) Roughly, how much have sheep and calves increased in weight?
   c) Apart from more meat, what are the other advantages of breeding bigger animals?
5 Read evidence C.
   a) Miss out the first of Young's seven points. Note down the other six. For each one, work out why it was an improvement and write down what you think the results were.
   b) Which do you think was most important?

A A picture of 1808, showing the new, bigger pig!

B The House of Commons was told about the increase in animal weight in 1795:

In 1710 the cattle and sheep sold at Smithfield Market weighed, on an average, as follows: Cattle, 370lb; Calves, 50lb; Sheep 28lb; Lambs, 18lb.
Now they weigh:
Cattle, 800lb; Calves, 143lb; Sheep 80lb; Lambs 50lb.

C Arthur Young helped to spread the new ideas by writing about them. In 1793, he became Secretary to the new Board of Agriculture. He described the changes in Norfolk in 1771:

As I shall presently leave Norfolk it will be proper to give a slight review of the **husbandry** which has rendered the name of this country so famous in the farming world. The great improvements have been made by means of the following circumstances:

First.	By enclosing without the assistance of Parliament.
Second.	By spirited use of marl and clay.
Third.	By the introduction of an excellent course of crops.
Fourth.	By the cultivation of turnips well hand-hoed.
Fifth.	By the culture of clover and ray-grass.
Sixth.	By the landlords granting long leases.
Seventh.	By the county being divided chiefly into large farms.

Enclosures

Farmers could make more profit if they used the new ideas and machines. But, in many areas, it was just impossible. Many villages still had large open fields around the village. They were divided into strips and villagers grew their own crops on their own strips. Their animals grazed on the common and wasteland.

One farmer could not experiment unless all the others agreed to do so, too. Above all, the system wasted time and land. The richer landowners wanted to change it.

The answer was enclosure. This meant dividing the land into separate farms, each surrounded by a hedge or fence. For years, some villagers had been swapping strips so that their land was not scattered about. Sometimes, they bought strips as well. In the 18th century, better-off farmers set about enclosing land in earnest.

If everyone agreed, that was fine. But if some of the poorer landowners objected, an Act of Parliament was needed. To get one passed, the owners of four-fifths of the land had to send a petition to Parliament. It cost a lot of money. However, if you owned enough land, it was worth it.

After the Act was passed, **commissioners** turned up to organise the sharing out of land. Each villager who owned strips was given one or more plots of an equal amount to his strips. Landowners were treated fairly. And, on their new enclosed fields, they could try out all the new farming ideas. They grew much more food to feed the growing population. They made more money.

But some villagers did not do that well out of enclosures. If you only owned a small piece of land, the cost of enclosing it was probably too high. You might have to sell up. If you could not prove you had owned your land, you did not get any after enclosure. Worse than that, you lost the chance to graze animals on the common.

So, many people became labourers. Jobs were often easy to get. The new farming methods actually needed *more* workers than before. A few people may have starved to death. Many others left their villages to look for work elsewhere.

One place to look was in one of the big new towns which were growing up. There were large factories in these towns, using new machines to make cloth. It was not just farming which was changing fast. Industry was going through its own revolution.

An open field village, showing the problems of strip farming.

A From 'A General View of the Agriculture of the County of Gloucester' (1807):

Aldsworth before Inclosure.

Management two shifts, crop and fallow.

Wheat, 200 acres, at 6 bushels per acre	150 quarters
Barley, 200 ditto, at 10 - - -	250 ditto
Oats, 200 ditto, at 10 - - -	250 ditto
Peas on fallow land called Etchings,	
100 - - 6 - - -	70 ditto
700 acres	720 quarters

Sheep bred, 200. Full stock, 400. Wool at eight fleeces per todd. 600 sheep taken to agistment, at 1s. per head.

Ten beasts bred and kept till four years old. Ten sold yearly, and forty taken to agistment, at 5s. per head.

After Inclosure.

Wheat sown, 390 acres	Produce, 585 quarters	
Barley, 390 -	- -	825 ditto
Peas & Oats, 390 -	- -	950 ditto
1170		2360
700 before inclos.		720 before inclos.
470 acres added		1640 quarters

Sheep bred annually, 1800. Beasts ditto, 12. Sent to market, several being bought in, 20.

One thousand eight hundred sheep, at five fleeces per todd, produce 360 todd, which adds 310 todds of wool after the inclosure.

B The number of enclosure acts passed by Parliament:

1720s – 25	1790s – 469
1730s – 39	1800s – 847
1740s – 36	1810s – 853
1750s – 137	1820s – 205
1760s – 385	
1770s – 660	After 1830, enclosure
1780s – 246	was on a smaller scale.

C Arthur Young described a Bedfordshire village, after enclosure in 1796:

The open field farmers had been very poor and backward and against inclosure but are now converted and admit the benefit of the measure. The value of sheep's wool is greatly increased. As to the **carcase**, the value is more than double. The new Leicester is seen.

The cottagers' cows are fewer but they have allotments instead. The land now produces more corn; the farmers are coming into better circumstances; the rent is raised; the poor are better employed. On the whole, the measure has been beneficial.

D William Cobbett described other villages in 1830:

The labourers' houses are beggarly in the extreme. The men and boys with dirty faces and dirty smock coats and dirty shirts. I have observed that, the richer the soil, the more miserable the labourers.

The cause is this: the great, the big bull frog grasps all. Every inch of land is [taken] by the rich. The wretched labourer has not a stick of wood and has no place for a pig or cow to graze, or even to lie down upon. It is impossible to have an idea of anything more miserable than the state of the labourer in this part of the country.

E A popular rhyme of the time:

They hang the man, and flog the woman,
That steals the goose from off the common;
But let the greater villain loose,
That steals the common from the goose.

1 Explain the meaning of each of these words: open field; strip; enclosure; commissioner; revolution.
2 Look carefully at the drawing on page 8.
   a) List all the ways in which land was wasted.
   b) Which do you think wasted *most* land? Give reasons for your choice.
   c) Think of at least two other problems about farming in this way.
3 a) Using the figures in evidence B, draw a graph to show the spread of enclosures.
   b) When were enclosures most common?
4 As a group, discuss evidence A.
   a) What are the main results of enclosure at Aldsworth?
   b) Explain why each of these groups of people benefited: (i) landowners; (ii) labourers; (iii) the general public.
   c) How can you tell that better sheep were bred after enclosure?
5 a) Read evidence C, D and E. For each one, write down whether the writer is for or against enclosure.
   b) Which extract do you think is most biased? Give reasons for your choice.
   c) In your own words, explain evidence D.

2 Changes in Industry

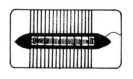

A CLOTHIER (RICH MERCHANT) BOUGHT THE WOOL FROM THE FARMER.

HE TOOK THE WOOL TO THE VILLAGERS WHO TURNED IT INTO CLOTH.

THEY DECIDED WHAT HOURS THEY WORKED.

THE CLOTHIER COLLECTED THE CLOTH AND PAID THE VILLAGERS FOR WHAT THEY HAD PRODUCED.

THE CLOTHIER TOOK THE CLOTH TO BE DYED, THEN SOLD IT.

spindle ley sewer patented pauper apprentice tow loom
cottage industry   domestic system
flying shuttle   spinning jenny   carding
spinning   weaving   spinning (water) frame
spinning mule   victuals

The Domestic System

Most of the goods we buy today are made by machines in factories. In 1714, most goods were made by hand in people's homes. The whole family joined in. Father, mother and children all had a part to play. Even three-year-olds could be expected to earn their keep.

Almost everything was made in this way. Buttons and nails, gloves and lace, were all made in people's own cottages. So we call this kind of industry the *cottage industry* or the *domestic system*. And the biggest cottage industry of all was the cloth industry.

There was a big demand for British wool abroad. In the main sheep-farming areas, there was plenty of work available, turning this wool into cloth. People worked long hours at this in dark, cramped rooms.

As the population grew, so did the demand for cloth. Cotton cloth from India had become popular. British merchants wanted to increase their profits by making more cotton cloth in Britain. They also wanted to keep prices down.

But the domestic system was slow and inefficient. So machines were invented to speed up production. It happened first in the cotton industry. Later, it would affect all industries. They were big changes; their effects were even greater. So historians call this 'The Industrial Revolution'.

The first invention came in 1733. A weaver called John Kay invented a 'flying' shuttle to speed up weaving. It meant the weaver could work more quickly and produce wider cloth. You might think the weavers would be pleased.

Not so. They were furious! It now took up to twice as many spinners to keep one weaver busy and weavers were afraid of losing their jobs. They wrecked Kay's house; they smashed up his machines. He gave up and fled to France.

The problem was that a spinner could only produce one **spindle** of yarn at a time. In 1764, another weaver called James Hargreaves came up with a solution. It was a machine which could spin eight threads at once, instead of one. This 'spinning jenny' was so simple that even a child could operate it.

Were the spinners pleased? No, they were furious! They attacked his house; they smashed his machines. He moved to Nottingham to get away from them. But the spinning jenny caught on quickly. By 1788, there were about 20 000 of them in use.

These machines did *not* end the domestic system. They were cheap to make and were powered by people. So they could easily be used in people's own homes. It was the *next* invention which was going to make people work in factories.

A Making woollen cloth involved many jobs: (1) *Carding* – taking the tangled wool and straightening it, often done by children; (2) *Spinning* – twisting the fibres into a single thread, often done by women; (3) *Weaving* – men turned the yarn into cloth on a **loom**.

B Samuel Crompton described the domestic system in the 1750s:

Soon after I was able to walk I was employed in the cotton manufacture. My mother used to bat the cotton wool on a wire riddle. It was then put into a deep brown mug with a strong **ley** of soap and suds.

My mother then tucked up my petticoats about my waist, and put me into the tub to tread upon the cotton at the bottom. When a second riddleful was batted, I was lifted out, it was placed in the mug, and I again trod it down. This was continued until the mug became so full that I could no longer safely stand in it. Then a chair was placed beside it and I held on by the back.

C Daniel Defoe described Halifax in the 1720s:

There are scattered cottages in which the women and children are always busy carding, spinning, etc. No hands being unemployed, all can [earn] their bread, even from the youngest to the ancient; hardly any [child] above four years old, but its hands are sufficient to itself.

D A report of 1840 on domestic weavers said:

The majority of cotton weavers work in cellars, which are seldom visited by the sun. The reason cellars are chosen is that cotton requires to be woven damp. The air must be cool and moist, instead of warm and dry.

I have seen them working in cellars dug out of an undrained swamp; the streets were without **sewers** and flooded with rain; the water running down the bare walls of the cellars and rendering them unfit for dogs or rats.

E Friedrich Engels looked back on the system in 1844:

Their children grew up in the fresh country air. If they could help their parents at work, it was only occasionally. Of eight or twelve hours' work for them, there was no question.

1 Write one sentence about each of these words: carding; spinning; weaving; yarn; loom; cottage industry; shuttle.

2 a) Explain how (i) the flying shuttle helped weavers and (ii) the spinning jenny helped spinners.
b) For each machine, explain why people objected to it so strongly.

3 Using only the picture strip on page 10, write down the advantages and the disadvantages of this system to the domestic worker.

4 Look at evidence A.
a) Write down what is happening at 1, 2 and 3.
b) Do you think it is a realistic picture? Give reasons for your view.

5 Read all the written evidence.
a) Which writer is in favour of the system?
b) Which writer is opposed to it?
c) What are your views about the work described in evidence C and D?
d) Is there anything in B, C or D which you think should not have been allowed?

THREE GREAT INVENTIONS IN THE COTTON INDUSTRY

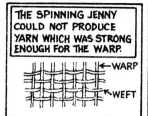

THE SPINNING JENNY COULD NOT PRODUCE YARN WHICH WAS STRONG ENOUGH FOR THE WARP.

←WARP

←WEFT

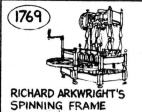

1769

RICHARD ARKWRIGHT'S SPINNING FRAME

COTTON MUST BE STRETCHED TO THE RIGHT THICKNESS BEFORE IT IS TWISTED.

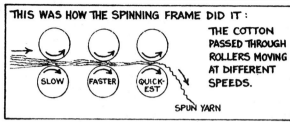

THIS WAS HOW THE SPINNING FRAME DID IT:

SLOW FASTER QUICK-EST

SPUN YARN

THE COTTON PASSED THROUGH ROLLERS MOVING AT DIFFERENT SPEEDS.

THE SPINNING FRAME COULD NOT MAKE FINE THREAD FOR EXPENSIVE CLOTH.

1779

A SPINNER CALLED SAMUEL CROMPTON SOLVED THE PROBLEM WITH HIS SPINNING MULE.

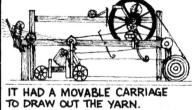

IT HAD A MOVABLE CARRIAGE TO DRAW OUT THE YARN.

PEOPLE SPIED ON HIM TO FIND OUT HOW IT WORKED.

THERE HAD NOW BEEN THREE SPINNING INVENTIONS IN A ROW...

WHAT WAS NEEDED WAS A MACHINE TO SPEED UP WEAVING.

1785

EDMUND CARTWRIGHT INVENTED A POWER LOOM...

...POWERED AT FIRST BY A HORSE.

LATER, WATER POWER WAS USED.

BUT THE LOOM HAD TO BE STOPPED OFTEN.

VARIOUS IMPROVEMENTS HAD TO BE MADE BEFORE..

...IT TOOK OVER FROM HAND WEAVING IN THE 19TH CENTURY.

The Factory System

More than anybody else, Richard Arkwright was responsible for the switch from home to factory production. He **patented** his spinning frame in 1769.

He could just have gone on building them and selling them, like Hargreaves with his spinning jenny. The spinning frame *could* have been made for use in cottages. People *could* have powered them themselves. But Arkwright was a clever businessman. Other early inventors were not.

Arkwright realised that his machine could be driven by other forms of power. He first set up a factory in Nottingham, using horse power.

Then, in 1771, he moved again. He built a mill at Cromford, near Derby. It stood beside a stream which joined the River Derwent. The idea was to use the water to work the machines. That is why his invention is often called the water frame.

Soon, about 300 people worked there; by 1789, it was over 800. In the mill, thousands of spindles were all spinning thread at once. By his death, Arkwright was running ten mills; he had made himself a fortune of £500 000. And the factory age had arrived.

Even so, most people were still working at home long afterwards. When Samuel Crompton invented his spinning mule in 1779, he simply wanted to use it at home. At first, it was not a factory machine. It was worked by hand and used by domestic workers in and around Bolton.

Even Cartwright's power loom did not immediately affect the land loom weaver. Early models were driven by horses or water-power. In any case, the machine had teething problems. Many changes were needed before it worked successfully.

In the 1790s, hand weavers, working at home, were still doing well. In 1792, Bolton weavers could be seen in town with £5 notes stuck in their hats. But hard times were just around the corner.

Within 30 years, hand loom weavers were finding it hard to compete with the power looms. Some of them had gone to work in the factories, along with their wives and children. One way of life was dying and something quite different was replacing it.

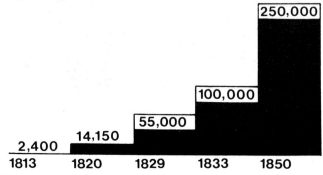

1813	1820	1829	1833	1850
2,400	14,150	55,000	100,000	250,000

The number of power looms in use.

An early mill. The captions explain how factories were different to the domestic system.

The labels on the drawing read:

- WORK DONE IN A SPECIAL BUILDING (A FACTORY)
- LARGE, SEMI-AUTOMATIC MACHINES
- FIXED HOURS OF WORKING
- EACH WORKER HAD A SPECIFIC JOB
- FIXED WEEKLY WAGE
- WATER POWER MEANT NON-STOP PRODUCTION WAS POSSIBLE
- OWNER WHO TOOK THE PROFITS

A   The loom on the right was made in 1710.

1   a) You will need to look back at pages 10 and 11 to answer this question. Divide two pages into five columns and put these headings at the top:
DATE; INVENTOR; MACHINE; WHAT IT DID; RESULTS.
In order, list the five main inventions and fill in the details in the columns.
b) Which inventions helped (i) spinning and (ii) weaving?
2   Draw a block graph to show the spread of power looms.
3   Look at evidence A. Write down what each person is doing in this photograph.
4   Look at the drawing above. Many hand loom weavers carried on working at home in great poverty, rather than work in a factory. Write down the things which you think they disliked about factory work. The picture gives you some clues.
5   Imagine you were one of the five inventors. Write a conversation in which you try to persuade a domestic worker to use your machine. Also, write down the sort of replies which you think the domestic worker might have made.

Work in the Mills

Much of the work in the mills was not hard but it did mean that people had to work at the machine's pace, not at their own. Hours were long; work was tedious.

The use of water power meant that many mills were built in the country. Often, there were not enough people living nearby to provide a work–force. One solution was to get **pauper** children from the towns. They worked as **apprentices**.

Some machines worked better if they were kept running. Water power made it possible to keep them going 24 hours a day, if necessary. So hours were long. A 14-hour day (including an hour for meals) was normal.

A child who looked after a spinning machine walked, backwards and forwards, about 40km a day. The temperature could reach 30°C. It must be stressed that conditions were *not* worse than in other industries. But the cloth industry was the biggest, so it got most attention.

A Robert Blincoe, aged about 7, was taken to a mill in Nottinghamshire. Years later, he described his arrival:

When the first cart drove up to the door, a number of villagers flocked round. Some exclaimed, 'God help the poor wretches.' 'Eh!' said another, 'what a fine collection of children; little do they know to what a life of slavery they are doomed.' 'The Lord have mercy upon them,' said a second. 'They'll find little mercy here,' said a third.

The other apprentices had not left work when this supply of children arrived. The supper consisted of milk-porridge of a very blue complexion! The bread was very black and so soft, that they could scarcely swallow it, as it stuck like bird-lime to their teeth.

B He also described his first meal there:

The room filled with a multitude of young persons of both sexes; from young women down to mere children. The boys generally had nothing on, but a shirt and trousers. Their hair looked as if a comb had seldom, if ever, been applied! The girls, as well as Blincoe could recollect, were, like the boys, [without] shoes and stockings.

The great bulk [of the apprentices] first looked after their supper, which consisted of new potatoes, distributed at a hatch door. At a signal, the apprentice rushed to this door, received his portion, and withdrew to his place at the table. Blincoe was startled, seeing the boys pull out the fore-part of their shirts, and holding it up with both hands, received the hot boiled potatoes. The girls held up their dirty, greasy aprons, that were saturated with grease and dirt. With a keen appetite, each apprentice devoured [ate] her allowance. Next, the hungry crew ran to the tables of the newcomers, and devoured every crust of bread and every drop of porridge they had left.

C Apprentices at Quarry Bank Mill in 1835:

On a sunny bank stands a handsome house, built for the accommodation of the female apprentices. Here, sixty young girls are well fed, clothed, educated and lodged. The female apprentices at Quarry Bank mill come partly from its own parish, but chiefly from the Liverpool poor-house. Their ages vary from ten to twenty-one years.

The apprentices have milk-porridge for breakfast, potatoes and bacon for dinner, and butcher-meat on Sundays. They have bacon every day.

D In 1816, Mr Moss, an apprentice-master, said:

Were any children injured by the machinery? – Very frequently. Very often their fingers were crushed, and one had his arm broken.

Were any of the children deformed? – Yes, several; there were two or three that were very crooked.

E A drawing from a novel written in 1840:

14

Read all the evidence before answering questions.

1 a) How did the treatment of the apprentices in evidence C differ from evidence A and B?
   b) List the evidence for ill-treatment.
   c) *Two* lots of people were responsible for punishing children. Who were they?
   d) Give reasons why *each* group should punish the children.
   e) Which example of ill-treatment do you find worst? Give reasons for your choice.

2 Look at evidence J. Write down what jobs you think the three numbered people do.
3 Why do you think that parents were keen to get their children jobs in the mills?
4 Imagine you were a reporter writing a news story about a mill. You may interview anyone you wish. Decide whom you would interview and write down all the questions you will ask.
5 Read page 94 carefully. As a group, discuss which pieces of evidence you think are most reliable.

F One man told a government enquiry in 1831–2 about his treatment some years earlier:

I was strapped most severely, till I could not bear to sit upon a chair without having pillows and I was forced to lie upon my face in the night time at one time. I was strapped both on my own legs and then I was put upon a man's back and then strapped. I was also buckled with two straps to an iron pillar, and flogged, all by one overlooker. After that he took a piece of **tow**, and twisted it in the shape of a cord, and put it in my mouth and tied it behind my head.

G More evidence from 1833. One way to keep young children working . . .

They used to ask the piecers if they'd mind their work and then they'd give 'em a halfpenny or a penny. Then the piecers was pleased, and worked; and if the piecers hadn't meat, they used to give 'em meat, and marbles, and tops; and at any pastime here gives 'em money; 6d or 1s [2½p or 5p].

H . . . and another way. Titus Bryan told a committee in 1819 about his daughter:

Have you a child of your own that scavenges for you: – Yes.
   Was the arm of that child ever broken? – Yes. How? – By a fall.
   Not in consequence of being beaten? – No, it was not by beating, it was pushed down, and her arm went down under her. It was me that pushed her down.
   Where did you take her to? – A doctor.
   How came you to push your child down? – It was for not just doing what I told her.

I A mill manager's view in 1816:

You have not observed that the twelve hours work has interfered with the health of the children? – I have not. I have seen many children that were taken in the works as young as six, whose health did not appear at all to suffer. On the contrary, when they [grew up], they appeared as healthy stout people as any in the country.
   Are the parents generally very [keen] to send their children to you? – Very.
   What are the weekly wages of a child of nine years old? – The children of 9 years are generally learners, and receive 7½p to 10p per week.

J Another scene from the 1840 book:

3 Coal Mining

Textiles were the key industry at the start of the industrial revolution. But coal was needed to keep it going. The early factories worked by water power; in the 19th century, they used steam instead. The steam came from burning coal.

Even in 1700, there was a growing demand for coal:

* people were using it in their homes;
* industry needed it: it was used in the making of soap, bricks, beer, sugar and glass.

The more people needed coal, the more the miners had to find. And the harder it got. For centuries, most coal had been mined as easily as possible. There were two main ways of doing this:

textile
fire damp   cavity   trapper

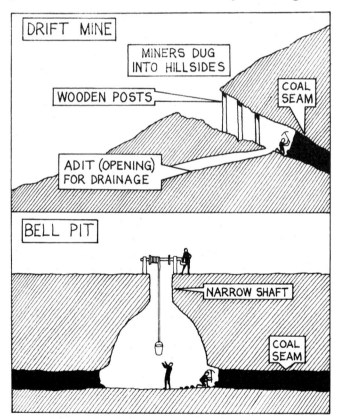

Neither of these ways produced much coal. During the 18th century, miners had to dig deeper to get enough. But, the deeper they dug, the more dangerous it became. The story of the coal industry is partly the story of how they overcame these dangers. The column opposite shows some solutions to these problems.

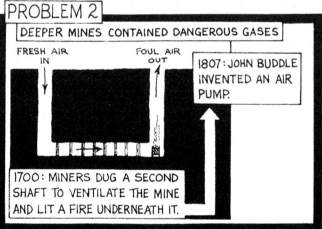

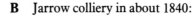

A A typical coal-mine in 1788:

B Jarrow colliery in about 1840:

C Another method of dealing with fire damp (methane gas). This man is dressed in wet sacks and carries a long pole with a candle on the end.

D This account from 1769 shows the dangers of fire damp:

Explosions from fire damp are well known wherever mines have been worked into a competent cavity [great depth]. One which happened near Newcastle was very remarkable. 70 men were blown out of the pit and a large piece of timber about ten metres long and 25 cms thick was blown a considerable distance and stuck into the side of a hill.

E Coal production figures:

1700 – 2.75 million tonnes
1750 – 4.75 million tonnes
1800 – 10 million tonnes
1850 – 50 million tonnes
1900 – 250 million tonnes

1 Divide your page into three columns and write these headings over the columns:
   DANGER; SOLUTION IN 1700; SOLUTION BY 1830.
   Using the column on page 16, list the dangers on the left and the solutions in the other columns.

2 a) Draw the diagram on the left on page 16.
   b) Why were deeper mines needed in the 1700s?

3 Look at evidence A. Note the date. Write down the numbers 1 to 4 on separate lines in your book. Beside each number, write down what each thing is and what you think it is used for.

4 Now, look at evidence B. Write down the differences between this mine and the mine in evidence A.

5 a) Look at evidence C and read evidence D. What do you think the man is doing, and why?
   b) Read evidence D again. Why do you think fire damp was a more common problem in the later 18th century?

6 From what you have read about mill work, do you think coal-mines would be worse or better places to work? Give reasons for your view.

Working in the Mines

Coal-mines made their owners rich. Even the workers were better paid than those working in the cotton mills. But working conditions were hard and dangerous.

Yet people outside the industry knew little about this. Mining villages were very self-contained; nearly everyone in them had a job connected with the mines. The villages were often rather cut off from the outside world.

The rest of Britain heard very little about coal-mines until 1842. In that year, Parliament published an enquiry into conditions in the mines. People were shocked when they found out what mining was really like. The pictures horrified them. Read the evidence for yourself, then decide what you feel about it.

All the evidence is from the Mines Report of 1842, unless it says otherwise.

A

B The youngest children, aged 5 upwards, were trappers. They opened and closed air-doors to let wagons through. Their pay was 2p a day for 12 or more hours' work. Sarah Gooder, aged 8, described the job:

It does not tire me but I have to trap without a light and I'm scared. I never go to sleep. Sometimes I sing when I've light, but not in the dark. I dare not sing then. I don't like being in the pit.

C

D In some mines, older girls carried coal to the surface in huge baskets on their backs. A leather strap round the girl's head held the basket in place. Sometimes, it was so heavy that their fathers hurt themselves lifting it on to the girls' backs. Ellison Jack, aged 11, said:

I have been working below three years on my father's account; he takes me down at two in the morning, and I come up at one and two next afternoon. I go to bed at six at night to be ready for work next morning. I have to bear my burden up four ladders before I get to the main road which leads to the pit bottom. My task is four or five tubs. Each tub holds 4¼ cwt [216 kilos]. I fill five tubs in twenty journeys.

I have had the strap when I did not do my bidding.

E

F Women were often employed to pull the coal wagons along the gallery. Each one could hold ½ tonne and they made 20 hauls in a shift. Betty Harris described the work:

I work from 6 in the morning to 6 at night. Stop about an hour at noon to eat my bread and butter. I get no drink.

I have a belt around my waist and a chain passing between my legs and I go on my hands and feet. We have to hold by a rope. When there is no rope, by anything we can catch hold of. It is very hard work for a woman.

The pit is very wet where I work and the water comes over our clog tops always. I have seen it up to my thighs. My clothes are wet through all day long. I have drawn till the skin was off me.

The belt and chain are worse when we are in the family way. I have had three or four children born on the same days as I have been at work and have gone back to work 9 or 10 days after. Four out of the eight children were still-born.

G   Winding children down into the mine:

H   G.W.M. Reynolds described girls' working dress:

Their dress is simply a pair of canvas trousers, supported by the hips and reaching a little below the knees. The friction of the chain constantly wears holes in the canvas, and leaves thighs bare. From the waist upwards, they are entirely uncovered; they work amongst the men, who are themselves [naked].

I   Causes of death in the mines:

Cause of Death.	Under 13 years of age.	13 and not exceeding 18 years of age.	Above 18 years of age.
Fell down the shafts	13	16	31
Fell down the shaft from the rope breaking	1	..	2
Fell out when ascending	..	..	3
Drawn over the pulley	3	..	3
Fall of stone out of a skip down the shaft	1	..	3
Drowned in the mines	3	4	15
Fall of stones, coal, and rubbish in the mines	14	14	69
Injuries in coal-pits, the nature of which is not specified	6	3	32
Crushed in coal-pits	..	1	1
Explosion of gas	13	18	49
Suffocated by choke-damp	..	2	6
Explosion of gunpowder	..	1	3
By tram-waggons	4	5	12
Total	58	62	229

J   Mine-owners complained to Parliament after the report was published. This was what they said about trappers:

The trapper's employment is not cheerless or dull; nor is he kept [alone] and in darkness all the time he is in the pit. An interval of seldom more than five minutes passes without some person passing through his door, and having a word with the trapper.

The trapper is generally cheerful and contented. Like other children of his age, he is occupied with some childish amusement – cutting sticks, making models and drawing with chalk on his door.

1   a) List all the dangers involved in mining. You should find at least ten. (Don't forget any mentioned on pages 16 and 17.)
b) Which do you think was most dangerous?
c) Some deaths were caused by carelessness. Why should the miners sometimes be careless?

2   a) What most shocks you, if anything, in this evidence?
b) What action do you think the government should take to change things for the better?
c) What do you think most shocked people in 1842?

3   a) Read evidence J. What differences are there between this and the other evidence?
b) Why is it different?
c) Which version do you believe, and why?

4   Why did (a) the adults and (b) the children put up with these conditions? Quote parts of the evidence to prove your answer.

5   Imagine you were a Member of Parliament in 1842. You have just read the report and want to get changes made. You decide to call a public meeting.
a) Design a poster to advertise the meeting.
b) Write out a brief speech you would make.

4 Making Iron

Industry needed iron. The early wooden machines were replaced by iron ones. Steam engines were made of iron. Nearly every industry used it. In the 18th century, more was needed than ever before.

The problem was making it. Iron ore comes from the ground but it has to be melted to get out the iron. This is called smelting. In 1700, **charcoal** was used to provide the heat.

But trees are needed for charcoal and supplies were running out. So cheaper iron was being **imported** from other countries. What the iron industry badly needed was a new fuel for smelting.

The man who discovered it was Abraham Darby, who owned an ironworks at Coalbrookdale in Shropshire. At first, he tried using coal. But coal contains sulphur and this can make the iron brittle.

Darby found that he had to heat the coal to turn it into coke before he could use it. In 1709, he at last found the right kind of local coal to make the process work.

Even then, he could only produce cast iron this way. It was his son, Abraham Darby II, who worked out how to use coke to make pig iron which was suitable for refining into bar iron. But many ironworks went on using charcoal for decades afterwards.

In any case, the method was not used for making wrought iron, which industry needed. Only in 1783 did Henry Cort of Hampshire patent his puddling process. At last, coke could be used. By then putting the iron through heavy rollers, he could produce a huge range of shapes.

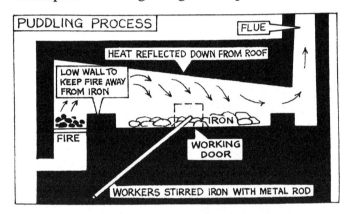

Other inventions followed. In the 19th century, men like Henry Bessemer made steel production quicker and cheaper. His 'converter' paved the way for a change-over. Many goods were now made from steel instead of iron.

However, it was men like Darby and Cort who made the discoveries which were vital for the Industrial Revolution. Their cheap iron was what British industry needed so badly.

HOW TO MAKE IRON

IRON ORE dug from the ground....

SMELTED in a furnace....

....makes PIG IRON. This is too hard to use as it is so it is either....

...SMELTED again and cast into shape in a mould. This is CAST IRON. Or....

....HEATED and HAMMERED, it produces a softer kind of iron – WROUGHT IRON.

CAST IRON is used for making things like CANNON and STOVES.

WROUGHT IRON is used for making things like TOOLS, MACHINERY and STEAM ENGINES.

A Making charcoal in 1763. This was how they did it: A clearing was made in the wood; a round hearth was made and a stake placed in the centre; wood was piled around the stake; the stake was taken away, leaving a hole to act as a chimney; this was covered with straw or brushwood, with damp earth on top; the pile was lit. After nearly a week, the charcoal was ready to be sold.

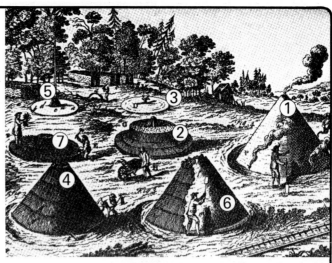

B Iron production went up fast:

1740 – 17 000 tonnes
1790 – 68 000 tonnes
1800 – 250 000 tonnes
1850 – 2 000 000 tonnes

C The works at Coalbrookdale in 1758.

1 Copy out and complete this paragraph:
  To make iron, iron ore has to be _____.
This is called _____. Charcoal was used as fuel until _____ when Abraham _____ first used _____ for smelting at his ironworks at _____. He used the process to make _____ iron and his son, _____ _____ II, used coke to make _____ iron.

2 a) In your own words, explain how Cort's puddling process worked.
  b) Look at the diagram at the bottom of the page. Which kind of iron do you think industry needed most? Give reasons for your answer.

3 a) Look at evidence A. Write down the numbers 1 to 7 on separate lines in your book.
  b) Read the caption and write down what is happening at each place.

4 a) Look at evidence C. What is being made at numbers 1 and 2?
  b) In which *two* ways can iron be taken from the works?
  c) What would the trees be used for? Why was this still needed in 1758?
  d) Do you think object 3 is going to or from the works? How did you decide?

5 New Roads for Old

A Roads could be *very* bad!

parish invested engineer
gradient
turnpike trust toll toll-keeper
camber tarmac

Goods such as coal and iron had to be carried to customers. Today, most of them would travel by road. In the early 18th century, the roads were too bad to do the job properly. They were more like rough cart tracks, filled with holes. And the country's traffic sank into them.

Each local **parish** was supposed to look after its own roads; each villager worked for six days every year, repairing them. But the villagers hardly used the main roads. So they weren't very worried about what they were like.

In 1663, Parliament tried a new solution. It passed a Turnpike Act. This allowed magistrates in three counties to charge travellers to use their roads. The money was to be spent on repairs. It was the first Act of many hundreds which were to cause a revolution in transport.

The great age of turnpike roads was the 18th century. Landowners and merchants asked Parliament to let them form private companies called turnpike trusts. The first one was set up in 1706. People **invested** money in these trusts and the money was spent on building a good road.

Gates were set up at intervals along each road. Travellers passing through a gate had to pay a toll to use the next stretch of road. Their money was collected by a toll-keeper and used to repair the road. Any profits went to the people who had invested in the turnpike trust.

People who had been used to travelling for nothing were not always pleased to have to pay, even if the road was better. Some people left the road to dodge the toll-gate; others tried to jump over it.

So the trusts had to use gates which 'turned' on a pivot. They also had 'pikes' (spikes) on top to stop people forcing their way through. These gates were called 'turnpikes'.

Of course, people still complained. In one riot in Wales, bands of men dressed up in women's nightgowns. Then, they attacked the gates and tollhouses. So Parliament passed a law which said that people who destroyed them could be hanged.

But most travellers were pleased with the roads. Merchants and manufacturers had most to gain. Their goods got to the customers more safely and more quickly. By 1830, over 35 400 km of roads were controlled by turnpike trusts.

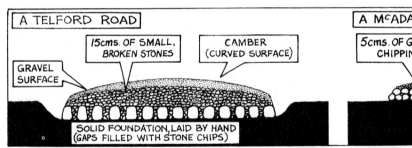

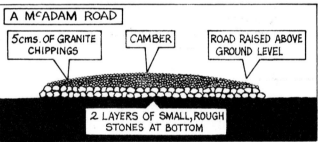

B The Tollgate at Tottenham Court Road. Look for: the toll-keeper's building; the board giving details of prices; milkmaids; various kinds of transport.

Two famous roadbuilders

Telford was a shepherd's son who began work as an apprentice mason. He went on to become one of the greatest **engineers** of his time. His training as a stone mason shows in the way he built his roads.

They were firm and dry, and lasted for years with hardly any repairs. But they took a long time to build and were very costly. Most of his roads were paid for by the government. Smaller trusts could not afford to pay him. But he built over 1600 km of roads. Their gentle **gradients** made them good for horse-drawn wagons.

McAdam made a fortune in America. Back in Britain, he invested it in his own system of road building. He believed that roads had to be dry and well-drained.

He was fussy about some details. All the base stones had to be broken up until they were roughly the same weight. He did not allow any earth to be added. He believed that the traffic would press down the top layer of chippings to form a smooth surface. He was right.

His roads were hard-wearing but not too costly. So his methods were in great demand. People wanted 'macadamised' roads. Years later, when tar was added, people called the surface 'tarmac'. We still do.

A TELFORD ROAD

GRAVEL SURFACE — 15cms. OF SMALL, BROKEN STONES — CAMBER (CURVED SURFACE) — SOLID FOUNDATION, LAID BY HAND (GAPS FILLED WITH STONE CHIPS)

A MᶜADAM ROAD

5cms. OF GRANITE CHIPPINGS — CAMBER — ROAD RAISED ABOVE GROUND LEVEL — 2 LAYERS OF SMALL, ROUGH STONES AT BOTTOM

1. Explain each word in the word box.
2. Answer these questions in complete sentences:
   a) In which year was the first Turnpike Act?
   b) When did turnpike trusts start?
   c) What did the trusts do with the tolls?
   d) What were the main benefits of turnpikes?
   e) Why did some people object to them?
3. a) Read this list of groups of people:
   merchants; farmers; farm labourers; tramps; the army; clergymen; rich landowners; long-distance lorry drivers; factory owners.
   b) Decide which groups gained by having better roads. In each case, give reasons why they benefited.
4. a) Look at evidence B. Write down the numbers 1 to 6 on separate lines. Beside each number, write down what you can see in the picture.
   b) In what ways is this road better than the road in evidence A?
   c) How were the new roads better for coach-owners?

6 The Canal Age

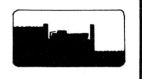

aqueduct
navigation   puddling   lock
canal mania

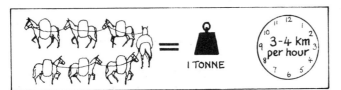

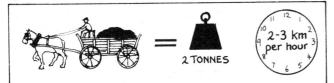

The turnpike trusts built many better roads. But horse-drawn wagons were still slow. The factory-owners of the Midlands and North really needed a faster, cheaper way of getting their goods to their customers.

They could use the sea – but only if their factory or mine was near it. They could use a river – but they might not be near that, either. Anyway, many rivers were too shallow. They just weren't good enough for carrying large amounts of heavy, bulky goods.

One person with just this problem was the Duke of Bridgewater. He had coal-mines on his Lancashire estate. If he could get his coal to Manchester quickly and cheaply, he stood to make a fortune. The problem was: how?

The Duke's answer was to build a canal. In 1759, Parliament passed an Act to allow him to build an 11-kilometre canal from his mines at Worsley, into Manchester. As his engineer, the Duke chose James Brindley. Brindley had done various engineering jobs before, but he had never built a canal.

It was all a great gamble. The Duke risked everything on the canal: he even borrowed £25 000. It was a huge sum for those days. Brindley's share was £1.05 a week in wages and free board and lodging.

Some people laughed at the idea and said it would never work. But Brindley proved the Duke right. The canal was finished in 1761. When it opened, people came from all over the country just to stare at it.

What really impressed them were two things. The first was the network of tunnels which Brindley had built right into the mines. But it was the second thing which caught people's imagination most.

At Barton, the canal had to avoid the River Irwell. Brindley's solution was an **aqueduct** which carried the canal over the river. People thought he was mad. When it was finished, they changed their minds. It was, they said, 'the eighth wonder of the world'.

The Duke had no doubts about its success. Brindley was soon building another canal for him. This continued the first canal from Manchester to Runcorn on the River Mersey. This canal could carry cotton from the port of Liverpool direct to the mills of Manchester.

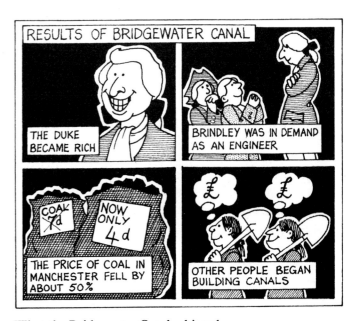

What the Bridgewater Canal achieved.

24

A The Barton Aqueduct. Notice the people on the towpath. Right: outline drawing of the aqueduct for question 3.

B Part of a letter written in Manchester, 1763:

Dear Sir,

I have been viewing the wonders of London and of the Peaks, but none of them gave me so much pleasure as the Duke of Bridgewater's navigation [canal] in this area. The ingenious but uneducated Mr Brindley has much such improvements as are truly astonishing. At Barton bridge he has erected a canal in the air. It is as high as the tops of the trees. Whilst I was surveying it with a mixture of wonder and delight, four barges passed me in the space of about three minutes, two of them being chained together, and dragged by two horses who went along the towpath. I dared hardly venture to walk [on this] as I trembled to behold the large river beneath me.

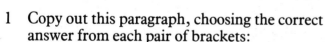

1 Copy out this paragraph, choosing the correct answer from each pair of brackets:

    The first important canal was built for the Duke of Bridgewater by James (Brindley/ Worsley). It was to carry (cotton/coal) from the mines at (Brindley/Worsley) to Manchester. It opened in (1759/1761). It included an aqueduct over the River (Erwell/Irwell) at (Barton/ Burton).

2 Look at the drawing at the top of page 24. Decide which of these goods you think canals were good for carrying:
coal; wheat; cattle; iron; milk; cotton; letters; turnips; manure; TV sets; cheese?

Write down those you choose. Then, explain fully why you rejected each of the others.

3 a) Look at evidence A. Draw the outline picture shown below it. Make it larger!
b) On your picture, label these features: a barge; the towpath; the aqueduct; the Bridgewater Canal; River Irwell; a mill.

4 a) Read evidence B. Which part of the canal is being described?
b) Which of these words describes the writer's feelings: bored; afraid; excited; sad; impressed; delighted; pleased; shocked? Give reasons for your choices.

Canal Development

Many other businessmen now wanted to invest in canals. Brindley himself went on to build nearly 580 km of canals, although few were finished before he died. His major work was the Trent and Mersey Canal, which he called the Grand Trunk Canal.

One of its main supporters was Josiah Wedgwood, a young man who owned a pottery works in Staffordshire. The canal brought clay to his potteries; and took his pottery to his customers. It was the start of a canal network.

But Brindley did more than this. He was the first modern British canal engineer. So he had to solve all the technical problems involved. Canals hold water – but water can drain away. Brindley had to work out how to keep the water in.

His answer was not a new one. He rediscovered the process of puddling. Workmen cut up slices of clay and mixed them with water. They then spread it on the canal sides and pressed it in.

There was another problem. Water flows downwards. So canals have to be built level or the water will just flow away. But Britain is a hilly country. Brindley's solution was to go round hills, if possible.

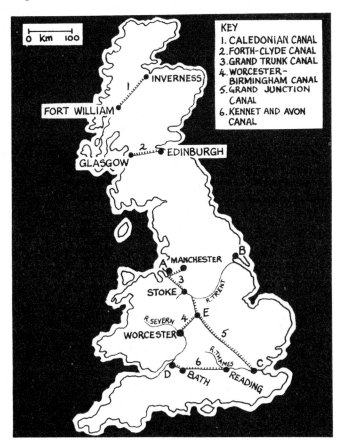

The main canals of Britain.

The other way was to build a canal in level stretches. At the end of each stretch was a system to lift or lower the boats. The simplest system is a lock.

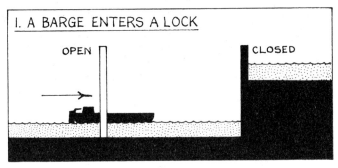

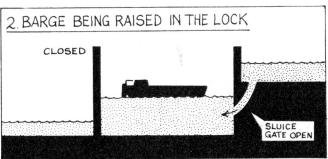

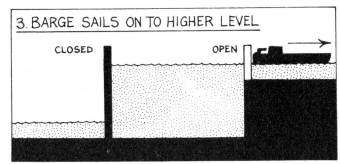

How a boat is raised in a lock.

Early canals made such good profits that people rushed to build more. The 1790s saw a period called 'canal mania'. People were keen to put their money into almost any new scheme.

Canals were ideal for carrying heavy and bulky goods, such as coal; fragile goods, like pottery; and agricultural products. They helped the building trade and brought work for the thousands of men who built them.

Above all, they provided the best way of carrying goods when Britain's industry was growing fast. It could not have made such rapid progress without canals.

They were most successful round about 1830. A decade later, there were over 6400 km of canals in Britain. But their great age was over. By then, a better form of transport had been found. It was the railway.

WHAT WAS WRONG WITH CANALS

CANALS VARIED IN WIDTH AND DEPTH

STAGECOACHES WERE FASTER. MOST PASSENGERS STILL WENT BY ROAD

ZZZZZ
SPEEDY GONZALES

CANALS WERE TOO SLOW FOR MAIL...

I'VE GOT LAST YEAR'S LETTER FOR YOU

...OR PERISHABLE FOOD

THEY COULD FREEZE UP IN WINTER...

...OR DRY UP IN SUMMER

A Tea-time on a monkey boat, 1874.

B George Smith campaigned for canal children:

I saw a boat cabin the other day in which there was only 202 cubic feet [5.7 cubic metres] of space. Living in it were a man, his wife and six children, one of the girls being 16 years of age, one 14, a boy of 10 and so on. A man, wife and 6 children and only one room.

I asked the woman how they slept. She showed me a table in front of the fire and said 3 children slept on that, 2 lay under the bed where the parents slept and two in a little cupboard above. The height of the cabin was only 5 feet [1.5 m].

C A Birmingham Factory Inspector said in 1875:

The women and children who travel with the slow boats do not receive wages. The father undertakes the care of the boat during the journey and makes use of his wife and children to assist in steering and following the horse on the towpath.

Children often commence to learn this work at the age of 6. The father's wages average £1 to £1.25 a week after paying the expenses of his horse. Of course, he has no rent to pay. In slack times, his boat may be tied up for a week while he earns nothing.

1 Explain each word in the word box on page 24.

2 a) Which of the following materials do you think were needed for *building* canals: timber; iron; cotton; bricks; plastic; stone; super glue; tiles; clay; pottery?
b) For each one you choose, write down what you think it was used for.
c) Was anything else needed?

3 a) Draw the map of the main canals on page 26.
b) Using a modern atlas, write in the names of the four ports (letters A, B, C and D).
c) Name city E at the heart of the network.

4 Look carefully at the lock diagram (page 26).
a) In your own words, explain how a lock worked.
b) Draw your own diagram to show how a boat was *lowered* from one level to another.

5 Look at all the evidence carefully.
a) How can you tell that evidence B is unreliable?
b) Do you think a boat child was better off than a mill worker? Give reasons.
c) What do you think were the disadvantages of the job?

7 The Power of Steam

bellows   furnace
cylinder   piston   condenser
flywheel   rotary steam engine

Water was the power which speeded up Britain's Industrial Revolution. By the 19th century, it was steam that was keeping it going.

Yet the first steam engine had been built in Devon as early as 1698 by a man called Thomas Savery. Ten years later, another Devon man called Thomas Newcomen patented the first practical steam engine.

It could only do a limited range of jobs. The main one was pumping water out of flooded mines. It could also work the **bellows** in a **furnace** at an ironworks. Abraham Darby II bought one to use at Coalbrookdale.

There were problems with Newcomen's engine, as you can see on the right. But solutions were found. For instance, the piston was kept tight with a layer of water above it.

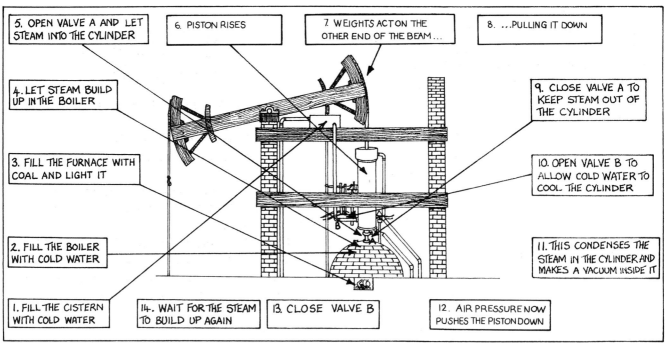

A step-by-step guide to how one of Newcomen's engines worked. The first one known to be built was in 1712. Its power was equal to about 5½ horse power.

The man most famous for making steam engines is James Watt. This is because he made the first really successful one. It was also the first to be driven only by steam.

In 1763, Watt was repairing one of Newcomen's engines and decided that he could make a better one. He saw that the cylinder had to be reheated each time to push the piston up. He realised it would be better if the cylinder stayed hot.

So he added another cylinder, called a condenser. The cold water condensed the steam in this one, instead of being sprayed on to the main cylinder. So the main cylinder stayed hot, which saved heat – and fuel.

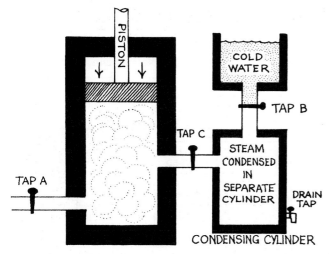

How the condensing cylinder worked.

In 1774, James Watt joined up with Matthew Boulton who owned a factory at Soho, near Birmingham. They began making steam engines. They were better than earlier ones but they could still only push up and down. This was all right for pumping water out of mines, but it was no good for driving machinery.

If he could invent an engine which could be used to turn a wheel, it could be used to power factory machines. In 1781, he succeeded. His idea was a simple one. The basic steam engine stayed the same, but he added a flywheel.

For the first time, steam *could* turn a wheel. A belt fixed to the wheel was linked to the machines in the factory. It was called the rotary steam engine. Within 50 years, it was operating most kinds of machinery. The age of steam had arrived.

This invention was so important because it was to change everybody's lives. One by one, the factories installed rotary engines. They worked best if they were kept going, so people worked long hours in the factories.

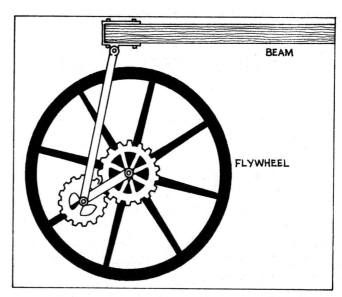

The rotary engine.

The more steam engines were used, the more coal was needed. So coalminers worked long hours in bad conditions to get it. Without the steam engine, there would have been no railway trains. And the railways changed everyone's lives, often for the better.

Above all, textile mills no longer needed to be near fast streams. New ones could be built in towns instead and large numbers of people moved to live there. Many must have thought they were heading for better times and a better life. When you have read the next few pages, you can decide if they were right.

1 a) Put these dates in order and write them on separate lines:
    1698; 1781; 1708; 1763; 1774.
   b) Beside each, write down what happened then.
2 What sort of jobs could these engines do:
   a) Savery's and Newcomen's; b) Watt's rotary engine?
3 a) Draw Newcomen's engine from page 28.
   b) In your own words, explain how it worked.
   c) Why was the condenser an improvement?
4 Think hard before answering this question.
   a) How did Newcomen's engine affect *coalminers*?
   b) How did the rotary engine affect (i) mill-workers and (ii) mill-owners?

terrace **dungheap**
back-to-back houses   courtyard
collier

Look at the figures opposite. They show how big some towns were in 1750 and how they grew over the next 100 years. See the huge difference.

The rich factory owners were proud of their new towns. They built public buildings, such as town halls, on a grand scale. They proved to everyone how wealthy the town was. In the back streets, however, things were very different.

People had flocked into these towns from the countryside. Towns seemed to offer guaranteed work and good wages; there was housing; there was work for the children. What more could a family want?

There was hardly any public transport so houses were built close to the factories, often by the factory-owners themselves. But land and houses cost money.

These houses were built as cheaply as possible. Rows of **terraces** were built back-to-back. It saved space and materials. Houses were built as cheaply as possible. But, after 1800, there just weren't enough houses to cope with the increasing population.

In hard times, people rented just one room of a house. Sometimes, two families shared the room. In 1847, up to 40 people were found sharing a room in Liverpool.

There were no indoor toilets in these houses; there was no piped water. The toilets and water tap were in a courtyard, which was shared by everyone living around it. Children played in it and people threw their rubbish there.

Often, it contained a large **dungheap** which might go on growing until a merchant bought it and carted it off. Sometimes, it was in an empty room of one of the houses instead. No wonder disease spread like wildfire.

The evidence on these pages gives you an idea of life in these towns. Each piece has been carefully dated so you can decide how long it took for conditions to improve.

A   Population increases in some British towns:

	1750	1801	1851
Liverpool	35 000	82 000	376 000
Birmingham	30 000	71 000	233 000
Manchester	45 000	75 000	303 000
Leeds	14 000	53 000	172 000
London	675 000	957 000	2 362 000

B   Back-to-back housing in Nottingham, 1845:

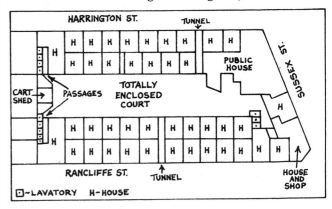

C   And in Leeds:

D   Average ages of death (from Chadwick's Report, 1842):

	Gentlemen	Labourers
Wiltshire	50	33
Liverpool	35	15
Manchester	38	17
Leeds	44	19
Bethnal Green	35	15

E Frying-Pan Alley, London, in 1862:

F Conditions in Liverpool in 1843:

Some time ago I visited a poor woman in distress, the wife of a labouring man.

She had been confined only a few days and herself and the infant were lying on straw in a vault through the outer cellar, with a clay floor impervious to water. There was no light nor ventilation in it and the air was dreadful. I had to walk on bricks across the floor to reach her bedside, as the floor itself was flooded with stagnant water.

G Lord Shaftesbury visited Frying-Pan Alley in 1847:

Frying-pan alley was a very famous alley in Holborn . . . In the first house that I turned into there was a single room. The window was very small and the light came through the door. I saw a young woman there, and I asked her if she had been there some little time.

'Yes,' she said, her husband went out to work and was obliged to come there to be near his work. She said, 'I am miserable.' 'What is it?' I asked.

'Look there,' said she, 'at that great hole; the landlord will not mend it. I have every night to sit and watch, or my husband sits up to watch, because the hole is over a common sewer and the rats come up, sometimes twenty at a time. If we did not watch for them, they would eat the baby up.'

H A workman's home in the 1880s:

1 a) Draw the plan of the back-to-back houses.
b) What is missing from these houses that we take for granted today?
c) Decide which house (or houses) would be worst to live in. Mark them with coloured crosses and give reasons for your choice.
2 a) Look at evidence H. How many people live in this room?
b) What do they have for sleeping?
c) What do they use for (i) light; (ii) heat?
d) What health risks can you see here?
3 a) Read evidence D. Using the other evidence, give at least three reasons why 'gentlemen' lived longer than labourers.
b) Now, give reasons why people lived much longer in Wiltshire than in Liverpool.
4 Which of the following reasons do you think explain the poor housing:
(i) the people living in them were poor;
(ii) houses were built as cheaply as possible;
(iii) good materials were not available;
(iv) the government did not insist on high standards;
(v) factory-owners did not care about the poor.
5 a) Which piece of evidence *proves* that the health risks were very great?
b) Which evidence most shocks or surprises you? Give reasons for your choice.
c) What, if anything, do you think the government should have done about it?

A One of the most famous street scenes is this one, called *Gin Lane*. Drawn by William Hogarth in 1751, it shows the dangers of drinking cheap gin. Gin-drinking actually went down towards the end of the 18th century, but was still common amongst poor people 100 years later. (However, even lemonade was alcoholic! It was made from equal parts of brandy, white wine and water.)

B An ex-miner said in 1842:

Many a collier [miner] spends in drink what he has shut up a young child the whole week to earn in a dark corner as a trapper.

C A London scene in 1834:

A woman almost in a state of nudity, with a fine infant at her breast, the only dress being its night-shirt, followed by another child about eight years old, a little girl without either shoes or stockings, followed a wretched-looking man into the house and remained there some time.

I saw them struggling through the crowd to get to the bar. They all had their gin. The infant had the first share from the woman's glass. They came back to the outside of the door, and there they could scarcely stand. The man and the woman appeared to quarrel. The little child in her arms cried: the wretched woman beat it.

After waiting for a few minutes the other little child ran across the road. The woman called to it to come back. It did so and she beat it. And when the children made so much noise that she could not [quieten] them, they all went into the shop again, and had some more gin.

D A report of 1852:

My father was a porter at the railway station and he came home drunk when he got paid, one Friday night. He took James and me, and he said he would take us to the canal and drown us. He told our step-mother to reach our shoes.

She said, 'If you are going to drown them, you may as well leave their shoes for Johnny.'

He took us, and he threw me in; and I should have drowned only for a boatman. There was two policemen on the bridge, with their lamps. They did not come to us then but they came to our house after we came home. They said they came to see about those two children; it was not a proper time to be on the canal side that time in the morning (2 o'clock).

Revision

1   This square includes the names of a number of people who have been mentioned so far. They could read up, down or sideways, as well as backwards. Each time you find a name, write it down and write one sentence, explaining why he was famous.

```
T U L L Y S B O W B
U L M C A D A M D U
S D A V Y D K Y N D
T A E E G R E L E D
R R O W N O W G H L
Y B O K U F E N S E
R Y E C O L L I N G
E L L O Y E L H W E
A Y A K T T A W O N
Y S S E T I R B T N
```

2   a) Read the bubbles carefully. Where are these children working?
b) What kinds of punishment can they expect?
c) What kind of work do they do?
d) Write an account of a day in the life of one of these children. Begin with the moment your parents get you up and include as much detail as possible.

3   Here are five sentences. Each has at least one spelling mistake in it. When you have spotted the mistakes, write them out correctly.
a) James Hagreaves invented the spinning jenny.
b) The Bridgewater Canal was built by Brindly.
c) James Watt invented the rotery engine.
d) Enclosures were worked out by comissioners.
e) Early industry was organised under the domestic systam.

4   How good is your memory? These two pictures are taken from pictures which have appeared earlier in this book. Here, you can see only a small part of the picture. It is a good test of how sharp-eyed you are! When you have found the original pictures, write down the page numbers where they appear.

The main problem was that the towns had just grown too quickly. No one had bothered to lay on proper services. The use of steam power added smoke and dirt, which made conditions even worse.

In many areas, there was no street lighting. Often, there were no sewers; the drains were open channels with dead animals lying in them. Most people got their water from the river or from a pump in the street. Dozens of families shared one pump – and one toilet!

Too often the water they used was **polluted**. The people of Reading and Oxford put their **sewage** into the River Thames; so did some Londoners. Then, other Londoners got the same water out of pumps in the street.

In these conditions, cholera became as common as plague had been in the Middle Ages. It first appeared in 1831. Those who caught it came out in black blotches; their lips turned blue; they were violently sick; and about half of them died. In 1848-9, over 50 000 people died from cholera. Some **cemeteries** had to be closed because they were too full.

Yet it was 1854 before anyone worked out that cholera was caused by dirty water. A London doctor called Snow found out that all the victims of one outbreak had got their water from one pump, in Broad Street. Even then, it was not until the 1870s that London's water began to be pure.

In 1842, a **civil servant** named Edwin Chadwick published a report which showed just how bad things were. He blamed the high death rate on:

* dirty air * polluted water * slum houses
* bad sewage systems * poor food

Parliament eventually took action. In 1848, it passed the first Public Health Act, setting up a Board of Health in London. This made it possible for any town to set up its own health board. However, it was not **compulsory** unless a town's death rate was over 23 people in every 1000. Some towns made huge improvements. In others, there were areas which were not much better in 1900. However, by then, at least cholera had almost died out.

A Jacob's Island in London.

B A description of Jacob's Island in 1874:

As we passed along the banks of the sewer, the sun shone upon a narrow strip of the water. In the shadow it looked as solid as black marble but in the bright light it appeared the colour of strong green tea.

We saw drains and sewers emptying their filthy contents into it. We saw a whole tier of privies [toilets, without doors], common to men and women, built over it. We heard bucket after bucket of filth splash into it. Yet, as we stood gazing in horror, we saw a child from one of the galleries lower a tin can with a rope to fill a large bucket that stood beside her.

slum   polluted   sewage
cemetery   civil servant   compulsory
cholera   night soilmen

C A Glasgow **slum** in 1868:

D The night soilmen who carted away the human dung could cause other problems (1845):

Nightmen are paid 15p for a load of 2 tonnes. To obtain this quantity, two men, with some assistance from their families or from the carters, may be able to load two carts from 3 a.m. to 9 a.m. They generally frequent those places where most manure is to be [got] with the least labour, neglecting to visit [other] districts.

The town surveyor of Liverpool states, 'Many of the privies are damaged by the nightmen breaking up the floors and seats to get out the soil. They will pull down one side of the bog-hole so that their work may be done with more ease. They cause considerable damage to property and it is too often left in the same state for a considerable time. The place becomes one open mass of filth.

E Problems of getting water in the 1840s. The first is from Bath; the second from Liverpool:

A man had to fetch water from one of the public pumps in Bath, about 400 metres away. 'It is as valuable,' he said, 'as strong beer. We can't use it for cooking, or anything of that sort, but only for drinking and tea.'

'Then where do you get the water for cooking and washing?' 'Why, from the river. But it is muddy, and often stinks bad, because all the filth is carried there.'

'Do you prefer to cook your victuals in water which is muddy and stinks to walking 400 metres to fetch it from the pump?'

'We can't help ourselves, you know. We could not go all that way for it.'

There is a good supply of water for the poor, if they had the means of preserving it. The water is turned on a certain number of hours during the day – four hours, perhaps. The poor go to the tap for it; it is constantly running. Each poor person fetches as much as they have pans to receive; but they are not well supplied with these articles, so they are frequently out of water. It is not sufficient for washing, or anything of that kind.

F The night soilmen.

1 Write one sentence about each of these words: sewage; cholera; night soilmen; polluted.
2 a) List Chadwick's five reasons for the high death-rate.
   b) A town council could have done something to improve *all* these things. In each case, write down at least one idea for making life better.
3 a) Look at evidence A and B. Explain in your own words why drinking water was polluted.
   b) Why did this increase the death rate?
4 a) Read evidence E. Give two reasons why the poor could not get enough water.
   b) Give *two* more reasons why it was polluted.
5 Look at evidence C. List the health risks you can spot in this photograph.

1755 TWO MEN STONED TO DEATH IN A LONDON PILLORY.

1837 PILLORY ENDED.

1757 WOMAN BURNED IN THE HAND FOR STEALING.

1831 BOY AGED NINE HANGED.

1868 PUBLIC EXECUTIONS STOPPED.

1841 CHILDREN AGED TEN TRANSPORTED.

1868 TRANSPORTATION ENDED.

There was a huge increase in crime during the 18th century. The big new towns made life easier for criminals. Many of them were never caught because there were no police to track them down.

Each parish had **magistrates**. Their job was to question suspects and try them in court. But they were not paid. Each parish also had a constable. He did the job for a year before someone else took over. But he wasn't paid either.

The bigger towns also had watchmen, whom people nicknamed 'Charleys'. Their job was to patrol the streets and keep a look-out for anything suspicious. They *were* paid, but it could be as little as 25p a week. So only people who could not get any other job took on the work.

In most places, they were a joke. They usually had a box somewhere on their beat where they could rest. Gangs of youths sometimes waited till the watchman was asleep there, then tipped his box over. One doctor even said that the best cure for anyone who could not sleep was to dress him up

magistrate   treason   heiress
capital crime   highwayman
'charleys'   transported   debtors
silent system   separate system
treadmill   guinea   Bow Street Runners

as a watchman. It would send him to sleep in no time!

So it is not surprising that few criminals were found. Because of that, the government made sure that those who were caught were punished severely.

Today, no criminal is hanged in Britain, even for murder. Yet, in the 1830s, a boy of nine was hanged in public for setting fire to a house. Punishments were as harsh as that.

In 1800, there were over 200 **capital crimes**. They included:
* murder, **treason** or piracy
* stealing anything worth 25p or more
* stealing an **heiress**!
* cutting down trees in an avenue
* shooting a rabbit

So hangings were common – and the public really enjoyed them. In London, they were carried out at Tyburn during most of the 18th century. Marble Arch stands there today. Huge crowds turned up: it was a day out for all the family.

Even so, far fewer people were hanged than should have been. Juries often took pity on young children and said they were not guilty, rather than have them hanged. Or they found them guilty of a less serious crime. Until 1868, many people were transported to colonies, such as Australia, instead.

Charleys got their nickname because they were started in the reign of Charles II.

A An execution at Tyburn.

B A description from the 1720s:

On the day of execution, the condemned prisoners are tied two together and placed on carts with their backs to the horses' tails. These carts are guarded and surrounded by constables and other police officers on horseback, armed with a sort of pike.

Tyburn is reached, and here stands the gibbet. One often sees criminals going to their death perfectly unconcerned; others fill themselves full of liquor. When all the prisoners arrive, they are made to mount on a very wide cart made for the purpose; a cord is passed round their necks and the end fastened to the gibbet. The chaplain who accompanies the condemned men is also on the cart; he makes them pray and sing a few verses of the Psalms.

The relatives are permitted to mount the cart and take farewell. When the time is up, the chaplain and the relations get off the cart, which slips from under the condemned men's feet. In this way, they remain all hanging together.

You often see friends and relations tugging at the hanging man's feet so that they should die quicker. The bodies and clothes of the dead belong to the executioner; relatives must, if they wish for them, buy them from him. Unclaimed bodies are sold to surgeons to be dissected. You see most amusing scenes between the people who do not like the bodies to be cut up and the messengers whom the surgeons have sent for the bodies; blows are given and returned before they can be got away.

1 a) Explain clearly why there were so many executions at this time.
   b) Why were fewer people hanged than should have been?
   c) Why were (i) Charleys and (ii) magistrates often unreliable? (Think carefully.)

2 Look at evidence A and read evidence B.
   a) Write down the numbers 1 to 6 on separate lines. Beside each number, write down what you can see in the picture.
   b) Look at the gibbet. Why do you think it is so large?

3 a) Read evidence B. The following events took place at an execution, but they are not in the right order. Choose the correct order, then write them out:

   prisoner stands on a wide cart; relatives say farewell; friends buy the prisoner's clothes; friends tug at the man's feet; the rope is put round the prisoner's neck; the cart is drawn away; prisoner is taken by cart to Tyburn.

   b) Which of these events do you find most surprising? Give reasons for your choice.

4 Look at the pictures at the top of page 36. Which punishment do you think was most unfair? What would a fair punishment have been?

Prisons and Reform

Most criminals spent some time in prison, even if it was only while they awaited trial. Nearly half the prisons were privately owned and their owners aimed to make a profit out of them. The conditions were dreadful.

About a quarter of the prisoners died each year from disease. Typhus was so common that people called it 'gaol fever'. Often, there was no proper water supply or sewage system. Visitors used handkerchiefs soaked in vinegar so they could not smell the prisoners; even judges were sometimes given nose clips.

The gaolers were not usually paid: they made their living out of the prisoners, by selling them food and drink. A rich prisoner could get almost anything he wanted – at a price!

Above all, the gaoler made money by charging fees. You even had to pay to get out of gaol. This was especially hard on debtors. They were people who were put in prison because they owed money.

One of them was John Howard, the High Sheriff of Bedfordshire after 1773. He was so shocked by what he saw that he tried to reform the prisons. He collected details about them and wrote a book called *State of the Prisons*; he also gave evidence to Parliament.

Other reformers actually went in to prisons to help the prisoners. One of these people was Elizabeth Fry who first visited London's Newgate Prison in 1813. She was so horrified by what she saw that she spent the rest of her life trying to improve prison conditions.

Elizabeth Fry was shocked by the dirt and by the prisoners' ignorance. She encouraged them to clean up their cells and she found them work, knitting stockings. Each prisoner could earn, on average, about 7½p a week doing this.

Debtors had to rely on charity.

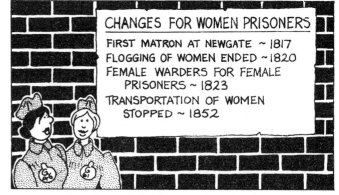

They could not get out until they had paid their debts – *and* paid the gaoler to free them. Many never did save up the money. They died before they managed it.

Most people accepted that prisons were awful places. They believed the criminals were wicked, so why should they be treated well? However, some people disagreed.

Above all, she helped the prisoners to read and write; she began a school for prisoners' children; and she held Bible readings. There were people who laughed at her ideas. But she did influence people's views on prison life. For instance, after 1820, women were no longer flogged as a punishment.

A Punishment for an 11-year-old in 1872:

HUNTINGDON COUNTY GAOL,

5th January 18 72

PARTICULARS of Persons convicted of an offence specified in the First Schedule of Habitual Criminals' Act, 1869, and who will be liberated from this Gaol within seven days from date hereof, either on expiration of sentence, or on Licence from Secretary of State.

Name and Aliases .... *Julia Oxgothorpe*

Photograph of Prisoner.

Description when liberated.

- Age (on discharge) *11*
- Height *4ft 1*
- Hair .... *D. Brown*
- Eyes .... *Grey*
- Complexion .... *Fresh*
- Where born .... *Nottingham*
- Married or single .... —
- Trade or occupation .... —
- Any other distinguishing mark ...

Address at time of apprehension .... *Grantham*

Whether summarily disposed of or tried by a Jury. *Summarily*

Place and date of conviction .... *Huntingdon 27 Jany 1872*

Offence for which convicted .... *Stealing Bread*

B A *later* account of what happened to Mr Arne, a debtor in the early 18th century:

On his arrival at the Fleet Prison, he was stripped naked and thrown into a dark dungeon just above the prison sewer. Occasionally, food was thrown down to him and a fellow prisoner, feeling sorry for him, found him an old mattress.

One Sunday, Arne escaped and ran towards the chapel while Sunday service was being held. The feathers from the mattress were sticking to his naked body, making him look like a 'repulsive bird'. He was taken back to his cell and locked up again.

C and D In the mid-19th century, two ways of dealing with prisoners were suggested. A book of 1861 described the Silent System and the Separate System:

The silent system is applied to a number of prisoners, varying from 40 to 80. They are seated upon forms, are about 3 metres apart, all facing in the direction of the officer's desk. All [are] employed in picking cotton, except a few who are undergoing the punishment of compulsory idleness. At meals, the same order is observed.

The discipline is not merely that the silence of the tongue is observed. No sign, no look, is permitted, nor is it often attempted. A prisoner, recently committed, and not yet quite sober, once started up with 'Britons never should be slaves'. A quiet smile on the face of some of the old gaol-birds was the only result: not a single head was turned while [he] was removed from the room.

As a general rule, a few months in the separate cell render a prisoner [easily persuaded]. The chaplain can then make the brawny navvy cry like a child; he can work on his feelings in almost any way he pleases. He can, so to speak, photograph his own thoughts, wishes and opinions on his patient's mind, and fill his mouth with his own phrases and language.

1 Answer these questions in complete sentences:
a) Why did visitors use handkerchiefs soaked in vinegar?
b) What was a debtor?
c) Why were prisons so unhealthy?
d) Why do you think that innocent prisoners were not immediately released, until 1774?
e) Which change for women prisoners do you think did the most good? Give reasons for your choice.
2 What did these people do to improve prisons:
(a) John Howard; (b) Elizabeth Fry?
3 Look at all the evidence.

a) Why did Mr Arne have his clothes removed?
b) How could a debtor make money in prison?
c) Do you think putting debtors in prison was a fair punishment? Give reasons.
4 a) In your own words, explain (i) the Silent System and (ii) the Separate System.
b) Which, if either, of the two systems do you think was best? Give reasons.
c) What are the risks of the Separate System?
5 a) Look at evidence A. What was her crime?
b) What do you think of her punishment?
c) Draw a wanted poster for this child, using the information in this evidence.

Police

London had the worst crime problem because it was the largest town. In 1750, a magistrate called Henry Fielding decided it was time to do something about it.

He gathered together six men who promised to serve for more than the usual year. They were paid a guinea (£1.05) a week and, later, given a proper uniform. Henry Fielding's office was in Bow Street. So this force later became known as the Bow Street Runners.

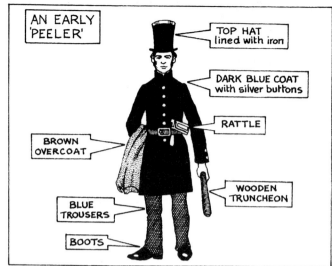

In 1763, Henry's blind brother John began a horse patrol to deal with **highwaymen**. It only lasted 18 months, although the idea was tried again in 1805.

Before that, Parliament had passed the Middlesex Justices Act in 1792. This Act set up seven other police offices in London. All of this was at least a start. But the country needed far more. It needed a proper police force.

The man who played a major part in creating it was Sir Robert Peel. It's unlikely he will ever be forgotten. People at the time nicknamed his police 'peelers' and, even today, we still call them 'bobbies'.

In 1828, Peel became Home Secretary so it was his job to deal with law and order. His solution was to form a better police force.

In 1829, he set up the Metropolitan Police Force to replace the Bow Street Foot Patrol. There were about 3000 men, under the control of two commissioners. These two men set up office in a building which had an entrance leading into Scotland Yard.

Many people were against the new police. 'Peel's Bloody Gang' they were nicknamed; some were jeered at or beaten up. Other people were afraid that the government would use the police as spies. But, gradually, they came to be accepted and people came to trust them.

However, these police only covered London; the rest of the country still relied on night watchmen. In fact, many towns saved money by having as few 'Charleys' as possible. If there was a riot, they simply called the army out.

Obviously, the government had to take a further step. The County Police Act of 1839 made it possible for county forces to be started.

Even then, many places still did not bother. So, in 1856, Parliament passed another act. The Rural Police Act made it compulsory to have police forces everywhere.

Essex was one of the first counties to set up a police force.

A These cases were all solved by 19th century detectives. Can *you* spot the tell-tale clues?

1 Major Hampton Lewis was asleep in his hotel room when he awoke to discover a man stealing his gold watch and purse. Although he chased after him, the man got away.

The Major called the police and told them his story, adding that it was a waste of time looking for any clues in the hotel. However, Superintendent Thomas made a thorough search of the room and found some small pieces of material.

Yes, said the Major, they were from the thief's shirt and braces which he had torn in the struggle. The thief had been in his shirt-sleeves. It was just the clue the Superintendent wanted.

2 In May 1840, Lord William Russell was murdered in bed in a smart part of London. He lived alone with three servants – a cook, a housemaid and a valet. When the housemaid got up at 6.30 a.m. and came downstairs, she was surprised to see how untidy the hall was. In the middle lay a bundle wrapped in cloth. The library was also in a mess.

She woke the other servants and they went to tell Lord William, only to find him dead. The police discovered that money, silver plate and jewellery were missing. They examined the bundle and found it contained a few little items, including a gold toothpick and a cook's thimble.

The back door had been forced and the front door was unbolted: it looked as though that had been the burglar's escape route.

But Inspector Pearce found that the marks on the back door had been made from the inside, not from the outside. He now had *two* clues. What were they?

At first, every policeman on duty had to wear a uniform. There were no detectives until 1842, after the police had bungled a murder hunt. (They had got their man, but only on the third attempt!) Policewomen did not appear until the 20th century, so policemen's wives had to do the job of looking after arrested women.

Policemen faced a tough life. They worked a shift system, including night work, seven days a week. Meal breaks did not exist: food and drink was carried 'on the beat' in a special blue bag. Some men even climbed gas lamps to heat up their tea!

Nor was the job itself easy. Policemen had none of the modern gadgets used to track down criminals. There were no radios; no police cars; no computers to store information. So detectives had to rely on common sense and experience.

B Fingerprint patterns. Fingerprinting was not used in Great Britain until the 20th century.

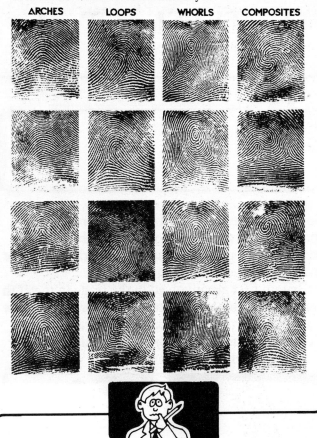

ARCHES LOOPS WHORLS COMPOSITES

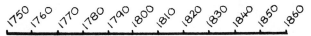

1 Draw a line 11 centimetres long and divide it up into centimetres. Each centimetre stands for ten years. Mark it as follows:

1750 1760 1770 1780 1790 1800 1810 1820 1830 1840 1850 1860

On this time-line, mark in the main events in early police history.

2 a) Explain why people were at first against having a regular police force.
b) Why were regular police better than
(i) 'Charleys'; (ii) Bow Street Runners;
(iii) the army? Give a different reason in each case.

3 a) Draw the picture of a Metropolitan policeman and colour it correctly.
b) Why do you think he had (i) a truncheon;
(ii) a rattle; (iii) a hat lined with iron?

4 Time to do some detective work of your own! Look at evidence A. Each part is a real 19th century case. Work out your solution to each mystery and write it down.

5 a) What type of fingerprint is yours? Which is most common in your group?
b) Explain how this discovery helped police.

41

11 The Slave Trade

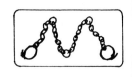

slave   dysentery   excrement

Some reformers achieved success more quickly than Howard and Fry. Long before the prisons were improved, Great Britain had ended the **slave** trade throughout her Empire.

Britain first got involved in the trade in the 16th century. By the 18th century, a trader could make a profit of up to £40 on each slave. Traders grew rich; so did the ports of Bristol and Liverpool.

This map shows how it worked:

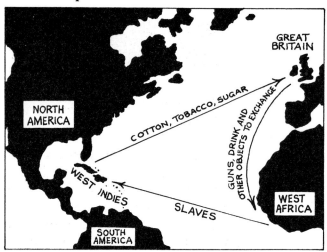

The Slave Trade, often known as the 'Slave Triangle'.

The middle part of the voyage involved the slaves. Once on board the ship, they were herded into the holds for a journey which took, on average, about five weeks. The men were chained up.

Many captains crammed in as many as possible. They knew a lot would die. They reckoned that, the more you started with, the more you would have left at the end.

Just twice a day, the slaves were taken out, exercised on deck and fed. Meanwhile, the crew cleaned up the blood and **excrement** from below decks. Even so, said one doctor, it was like a slaughter-house. You could smell a slave ship from 8 km away.

Some slaves went mad and were killed by the crew; others killed themselves. Diseases like smallpox and **dysentery** could wipe out 25% of the slaves before the journey was over. Even those who were infected, but still alive, were usually thrown overboard.

Once ashore in the West Indies, the slaves were put up for sale. The best slaves would fetch £60 or more each; others went for just a pound or two; the weakest of all were left to die on the waterfront.

Those who lived did not find an easy life waiting for them. Most worked on sugar-cane plantations from sunrise to sunset – an endless round of work and ill-treatment.

In the second half of the 18th century, pressure grew to end the slave trade. An Anti-Slavery Movement was formed to persuade people that slavery was wrong. It was a hard job. Many people made a lot of money from the trade; captains fought hard to keep it going.

Just some of the devices used to punish slaves.

Inventory &c Continued

Negroes

Names	Employment and Discription	Price
Jimmy	A compt mill Carpenter &c in his time	£ 330
Yankey	Mill boatswain & half bred Carpenter old	50
Cubbena	A Good mason workman healthy and Young	150
Guy	A well disposed promising Lad A mason	100
Billy	A Good workman A mason	115
Butler	Very Indifferent fellow with bad Legs	6
Ceasar	A Good and Intelligent Driver Carter &c	150
Arajuna	A Good driver Mill feeder &c	155
Rickard	Mill feeder and Carter fencible knowing	100
Primas	An Excellent Tradesman boiler Ruptured old	25
Broomer	Ditto and finer in prime of Life	165
James	Ditto an Intelligent Good fellow	165
Quacoe	An Excellent Carter and knowing about Cattle	125

Slave prices in 1787.

One of the movement's leaders was Thomas Clarkson. His job was to find out as much as possible about the trade. He talked to sailors; he inspected ships; he even bought objects such as thumb screws which were used to punish slaves.

Another key member was an MP called William Wilberforce. His job was to persuade the House of Commons to end the trade. It took nearly 20 years.

At last, in 1807, Parliament banned the sale of slaves throughout the Empire. This did not mean the end of slavery itself: that went on until 1833. But, after 1807, it was illegal for a British person to buy or sell another human being. It still is, today.

Wedgwood's wax seal, made as publicity against the trade.

1 Copy out and complete this paragraph:
The Anti-Slavery _____ was formed in the second half of the ___ century to persuade people that slavery was wrong. Thomas ___ had the job of finding out about the trade. An MP, William ___, tried to persuade Parliament to end the trade. It was finally ended in _____, although _____ itself did not end until 1833.

2 Which pictures on these pages do you think are evidence? Give reasons for your choices.

3 a) Look at the picture above and work out what it says. Give reasons why some slaves, such as Jimmy, fetched high prices.
b) Why was Butler sold so cheaply?
c) If the ship had landed about 300 slaves and these were typical prices, roughly how much would the captain make?

4 a) Look at the picture of the wax seal. What is the slave doing in the picture?
b) Write down what it says on the seal. What do you think it means?

5 *Either* write a short speech against the slave trade *or* design your own wax seal.

shearing machine

The Luddites

The government was ready to help the slaves overseas but it took a different view of the poor in Britain. Instead of helping them, the government passed tougher laws to keep them under control. The worst problems were in the North and Midlands.

In the Midlands, there was a big cottage industry in knitting stockings. In 1800, a hand knitter could earn up to £1.35 a week. But factory-owners were installing new machines which could make wider cloth. This was then cut up to make stockings.

It was poorer quality – but it was cheaper. The cottage workers just could not compete; their wages fell sharply, while food costs were rising.

So the cottage workers fought back. In 1811, organised gangs set about smashing the new machines. In one year alone, they destroyed about 1000 of them.

These gangs were called 'Luddites'. The story was that they were led by someone called Ned Ludd, who lived secretly in Sherwood Forest. If he did, no one ever found him!

By the spring of 1812, the violence had spread. In Lancashire, the target was the power loom; in Yorkshire, Luddites went for **shearing machines**.

Whatever the target, the pattern was much the same. The gangs struck at night, under cover of darkness. There was no police force and local constables could not cope.

A A Luddite attack.

Britain was at war with France at the time. No country at war can also put up with riots at home. So the government took stern action over the Luddites and brought in soldiers to help defend the factories.

The result was armed fights. In 1812, about 150 Luddites attacked William Cartwright's mill near Huddersfield. But the mill-owner was prepared and soldiers opened fire on the mob, killing two of them.

That same year, the government made machine-wrecking a capital crime. In 1813, 14 of the Luddites who had attacked Cartwright's mill were hanged.

The harsh punishments worked. The riots became fewer, although they did not end. In later years, attacks were still made occasionally. But the machines stayed. The Luddites were beaten – and got poorer.

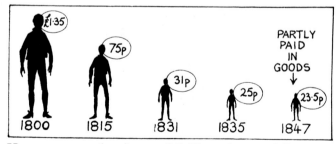

How cottage workers' wages fell. Hours increased. By 1835, a 90-hour week was common.

To Mr Smith Shearing Frame Holder at Hill End Yorkshire

Sir

Information has just been given in that you are a holder of those detestable Shearing Frames, and I was desired by my Men to write to you and give you fair Warning to pull them down, and for that purpose I desire you will now understand I am now writing to you you will take Notice that if they are not taken down by the end of next Week, I will detach one of my Lieutenants with at least 300 Men to destroy them and furthermore take Notice that if you give us the trouble of coming so far we will increase your misfortune by burning your Buildings down to Ashes and if you have impudence to fire upon any of my men, they have orders to morder you and burn all your Housing, you will have the Goodness to your Neighbours to inform them that the same fate awaits them if their Frames are not speedily taken down as I understand their are several in your Neighbourhood. Frame Holders. And as the views and Intentions of me and my Men have been much misrepresented I will take this opportunity of stating them, which I desire you will let all your Brethren in Sin know of....

B A letter from Ned Ludd.

C A writer described how special constables were called out to help deal with Luddites (1867):

Their daring and courage were shown in the instance of one [Luddite] who entered a house alone in Rutland Street, Nottingham, one evening. [He] proceeded upstairs and smashed the material parts of a frame in a minute or two. But that short time was sufficient to cause an alarm; constables were in front of the house.

The man at once saw his danger, threw himself on the roof. Passing along others, he saw in the dim light that the earth had been lately dug in a garden below, and leaped from the house upon it. The frame-breaker quietly passed through a kitchen where a family were at table, and escaped. In a few minutes, the shouts of a sympathising crowd were heard 1/3 km away.

D Richard Oastler described hand-loom weavers (1830s):

They were making from 22½ to 26p a week clear wages. I very often find them going home without work at all. There are hundreds of families in the district to whom a piece of flesh meat is a luxury; it does not form a regular article in their daily diet. They generally live upon porridge and potatoes. As to their clothing, they are clothed in rags.

E A framework knitter:

Her age she stated to be 53; she had the appearance of being 70; there were bones, sinews and skin, but no appearance of flesh. She had been the mother of fifteen children, ten of whom had become stockingers. From sickness in a morning, she could not work before her breakfast of tea, but laboured at night till ten o'clock, and her clear earnings were about 12½p weekly. The rent of [the frame] was 7½p a week. The house rent was 12½p a week. It was ill-drained, damp and unhealthy. [Despite this, nothing persuaded] her husband to send his children into any better paid and more promising occupations. They seem to have had the idea that, having come from a framework-knitting family, they must forever remain in that job.

1 Answer these questions in complete sentences:
   a) Who were the Luddites?
   b) When, and where, did Luddite riots happen?
   c) Why did Luddites smash up machinery?
   d) What *two* actions did the government take to stop the riots?

2 a) Look at evidence A. What *five* weapons are the men carrying?
   b) What do you think the women are doing?
   c) Read evidence B. What threats are made?
   d) Which county did this letter come from?

(Clue: read the first sentence carefully.)

3 a) Read evidence C. How is this attack different from that in evidence A?
   b) Has this Luddite attacked a factory or not? Explain how you decided.

4 a) Read evidence E. What signs of poverty are there in this woman's home?
   b) The writer does not blame machines for causing the knitters' poverty. What reason does he give?
   c) Why do you think they go on putting up with living in poverty?

> **threshing machine** **poaching**
> **arson** **workhouse** man-trap

Captain Swing

In 1815, Britain came to the end of a long period of wars against France. The government was afraid that corn prices would fall so it passed a Corn Law to protect farmers. Even so, corn prices still fell.

Farmers made less profit so they paid their workers lower wages. They also bought new machinery, such as **threshing machines**. Farm workers now faced the sack in the winter months when before they would have been threshing.

These workers were already desperately poor. Pay was low and there was a lot of unemployment. It was also difficult to get extra food: anyone found guilty of **poaching** could be transported.

The Luddites had attacked factory machines; now, farm workers did the same to threshing machines. Violence and riots rapidly spread over the Midlands, East Anglia and southern England.

Labourers burned down hay ricks and destroyed the machines; they attacked workhouses; they sent threatening letters to farmers. Often, letters were signed by 'Captain Swing'. It is unlikely he existed, any more than Ned Ludd did.

The first machine-breakers got off lightly; later, the government took a tough line. In November 1830, it offered £500 reward for information which would lead to arrests. Within weeks, the worst of the attacks were over.

The courts dealt severely with those who were found guilty. Nearly 2000 people were put on trial. Sentences included:

* 19 people hanged, mostly for **arson**
* 644 put in prison
* 481 transported to Australia

Afterwards, in some areas, wages *were* raised. And many farmers *did* get rid of their threshing machines. However, the problem of poverty remained. Many labourers and their families wound up in **workhouses**. They were kept in them, they said, 'like potatoes in a pit', only being taken out when farmers needed workers.

Even after 1850, when British farming enjoyed a 'golden age' of high profits, farm workers were low paid. After 1875, British farmers had to compete with imported food. There was a depression in agriculture. Between then and 1900, one-third of farm labourers had left the land.

A   A Hampshire labourer said how he got involved:

Oh, I wor with them. But then, everybody was forced like to go. There was no denying. I be an old man now. I was not young then. It was the little men as did it. They worked, you see, for little wages, as they do now. They suffers most. They get but 20p, 22½p and 25p. One or two may get 27½p a week.

I was took afore Squire Wickham and the other gentlemen, for the squire to shew as how I had no business to be mobbing. I was a hurdle maker and thatcher, and jobbed at hedging. The squire shewed as how I got £64 a year from him for work of that kind. But he did not show that I had most times a man to help me, and two women at times. He did not show that I paid as much as £20 some years for helpers.

B   A Swing letter. (Two and sixpence = 12½p.)

> this is to inform you what you have to undergo Jentelmen if providing you Dont pull down your meshines and rise the poor mens wages the maried men give tow and six pence a day a day the singel tow eshilings. or we will burn down your barns and you in them this is the last notis
>
> from W Sk

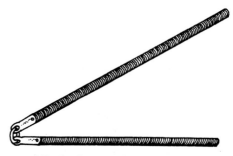

The name of 'Swing' may refer to the flail used in threshing. When it is used, the stick swings.

C One threshing machine could cost 15 men their jobs in the winter.

D Scenes from a labourer's life in the 1830s:

Sugar was so coarse and black that, when used, it turned water black. Bread had to be bought and consumed by the working classes, but butter was very seldom used owing to its cost. Black treacle was used in the place of butter or lard. This stuff was spread in almost invisible thinness over the always short weight bread.

The bread was not always made of wheat. It was sometimes made up from rye and barley. This coarse brown bread was termed 'rangatang' by our forefathers. At times, labouring folks had 'cakes'. These cakes were hard pieces of dough, baked over a hearth, and they had smoke for a tasty flavouring.

Our grandfathers and grandmothers made tea when they could get it, as follows. Bread was toasted until it became black and hard. In this condition, it was grated into hot water, in which a minute pinch of tea was added from a ¼ oz [7 g] packet.

E From *The Examiner*, February 1831:

Ye Gods above, send down your love,
With swords as sharp as sickles,
To cut the throats of gentlefolks,
Who rob the poor of victuals.

Now you little rascal, I'll give you your choice either to stop by your handy work and be roasted, or come with me and be hanged a little bit.

F Cartoon showing the Duke of Wellington talking to a rioter. Notice the man-trap for catching poachers.

1 Copy out and complete this paragraph:
In ___, farm workers in the Midlands, East ___ and the south began rioting. They destroyed the ___ machines which had put them out of work in the ___ months. These riots are called the ____ riots. They probably got their name from the swinging stick of the ____ used in threshing.

2 Look at all the evidence on these two pages.
a) In evidence C, what 'weapons' are the men using? What *else* could they have used?
b) Write down what you think evidence B says.
c) What, exactly, does the writer threaten?

3 a) Did the writer of evidence A want to join the rioters? How do you know?
b) How much did the squire say the man earned in a *week*?
c) Why did the man think the squire's way of looking at it was unfair?

4 a) In evidence F, what two choices does the Duke offer the rioter? Explain your answer.
b) Which pieces of evidence sympathise with the rioters?

5 You and your parents could try making tea in the way described in evidence D. Then, write down what you learn from the experience!

trade union   friendly society
initiation ceremony   poor relief

GEORGE LOVELESS, AGED 41

The Tolpuddle Martyrs

The Luddites had not had a chance to join a **trade union** because unions were banned after 1800. The government had been frightened that they could be dangerous. But, in 1824, Parliament had passed a law to make them legal again. Ten years later, the Grand National Consolidated Trades Union was formed. It was the biggest union yet, with half a million members.

News of this union reached Dorset, where the farm labourers were desperately poor. In the village of Tolpuddle, their pay was only 35p a week, 15p less than elsewhere. And farmers were planning to bring it down to just 30p.

One worker called George Loveless decided that he would start a **friendly society**. Although this was not against the law, he thought it would be better to keep it secret. After all, the farmers might choose to sack any workers who belonged to it.

It cost 5p to join the union and ½p a week after that. To be on the safe side, they met at night. Also, new members had to join in an **initiation ceremony** and swear an oath.

The government was looking for ways to deal with trades unions and the Tolpuddle labourers gave them their chance. Trades unions were not illegal but there was a law against making secret oaths. It had been passed back in 1797.

Early on February 24th 1834, the local constable arrested George Loveless and six other men. They were marched 11 kilometres to Dorchester and put in prison. They were charged with swearing a secret oath.

In court, George Loveless told the magistrates that they had not intended to do any harm. They just wanted to stop their families from starving. It did no good. The judge told them that he was sentencing them 'as an example to the working class'. Each prisoner got the same sentence: seven years' transportation to Australia.

It meant leaving their families behind and it was unlikely that they would ever afford to come back. After they had gone, their wives were not even given **poor relief**. They were told that, if their husbands could afford to join a union, they could afford to look after their families!

Yet they did come back. There was such a public outcry that Parliament had to think again. In 1837, the men were given a free passage home.

However, the memories of it all stayed. People were frightened to join the unions for many years afterwards. Instead, workers looked for some other way to improve their lives.

The sign of the 'Martyrs Inn' at Tolpuddle today.

JAMES BRINE, AGED 25

THOMAS STANFIELD, AGED 51

JOHN STANFIELD, AGED 25

JAMES LOVELESS, AGED 29

A   This article appeared in the *London Satirist* (1838):

The Portraits.

We this week present our readers with the portraits of the five Dorchester labourers who have returned to their country after a cruel, and is now admitted, an unjustifiable expatriation of some years. The sixth "convict" is still in the land of his exile, and though excluded from our picture gallery, is not shut out from our sympathies and affections. The following is George Loveless's relation of their trial, taken from his pamphlet "Victims of Whiggery," which we again earnestly recommend to all our readers and friends :—

On the 15th of March, we were taken to the County-hall to await our trial. As soon as we arrived we were ushered down some steps into a miserable dungeon, opened but twice a year, with only a glimmering light ; and to make it more disagreeable, some wet and green brushwood was served for firing. The smoke of this place, together with its natural dampness, amounted to nearly suffocation ; and in this most dreadful situation we passed three whole days. As to the trial, I need mention but little ; the whole proceedings were characterised by a shameful disregard of justice and decency ; the most unfair means were resorted to in order to frame an indictment against us ; the grand jury appeared to ransack heaven and earth to get some clue against us, but in vain ; our characters were investigated from our infancy to the then present moment ; our masters were inquired of to know if we were not idle, or attended public-houses, or some other fault in us ; and much as they were opposed to us, they had common honesty enough to declare that we were good labouring servants, and that they never heard of any complaint against us ; and when nothing whatever could be raked together, the unjust and cruel judge, John Williams, ordered us to be tried for mutiny and conspiracy, under an act 37 Geo. III., cap. 123, for the suppression of mutiny amongst the marines and seamen, several years ago, at the Nore. The greater part of the evidence against us, on our trial, was put into the mouths of the witnesses by the judge ; and when he evidently wished them to say any particular thing, and the witness would say, "I cannot remember," he would say, "Now think : I will give you another minute to consider;" and he would then repeat over the words, and ask, "Cannot you remember ?" Sometimes, by charging them to be careful what they said, by way of intimidation, they would merely answer "Yes ;" and the judge would set the words down as proceeding from the witness. I shall not soon forget his address to the jury, in summing up the evidence: among other things he told them, that if such Societies were allowed to exist, it would ruin masters, cause a stagnation in trade, destroy property, and if *they should not* find us guilty, *he was certain they would forfeit the opinion of the grand jury.* I thought to myself, there is no danger but we shall be found guilty, as we have a special jury for the purpose, selected from among those who are most unfriendly towards us—the grand jury, landowners, the petty-jury, land-renters. Under such a charge, from such a quarter, self-interest alone would induce them to say "Guilty." The judge then inquired if we had anything to say ? I instantly forwarded the following short defence, in writing, to him :—"My Lord, if we have violated any law, it was not done intentionally ; we have injured no man's reputation, character, person, or property ; we were uniting together to preserve ourselves, our wives, and our children, from utter degradation and starvation. We challenge any man, or number of men, to prove that we have acted, or intend to act, different from the above statement." The judge asked if I wished it to be read in court. I answered, "Yes." It was then mumbled over to a part of the jury, in such an inaudible manner, that although I knew what was there, I could not comprehend it. And here one of the counsel prevented sentence being passed, by declaring that not one charge brought against any of the prisoners at the bar was proved, and that if we were found guilty a great number of persons would be dissatisfied ; "and I shall for one," said he.

1   This paragraph about the labourers contains some mistakes. Copy it out, correcting the mistakes as you go along.

   The Great National Consolidated Trades Union was formed in 1834. Some labourers at Tolpuddle organised their own union, led by George Hateless. Six of the members were arrested for swearing on a bus and were sentenced to a holiday in Australia.

2   Look at evidence A. You may need a dictionary to follow the text.
   a) Is this biased for or against the men? Write down how you worked this out.
   b) According to Loveless, how did the judge show that *he* was biased against the men?

3   a) Why was it a punishment to be transported?
   b) Do you think the men's families were treated fairly? Give reasons for your view.

4   a) Why do you think people often call these men 'The Tolpuddle *Martyrs*'?
   b) Look at the photograph of the inn sign. Design your own sign which would be suitable for the 'Martyrs' Inn'.

The Chartists

Some workers thought that what they needed was the right to vote in elections for members of Parliament. Then, they would be able to influence Parliament to improve their lives.

In the 18th century, hardly any poor people could vote. Mostly, it was only those who owned property who were able to vote. In some places, the landowner just picked whoever he wanted as MP. They called these places 'rotten boroughs'. While they *did* have MPs, many of the big new industrial towns had no MP at all. It was clearly unfair.

> YOU CAN'T ALL BE FLOATING VOTERS!

One of the most rotten of the 'rotten boroughs' was Dunwich in Suffolk. It had disappeared beneath the sea long before.

In 1832, Parliament at last passed a Reform Bill to improve the situation. Many of the rotten boroughs lost their MPs and new towns were given them instead. More people were allowed to vote.

The working class had fought hardest for these changes; they had led the rioting and held protest demonstrations. Yet the new Act gave them nothing: it was the **middle classes** who were given the vote, not the workers. Not surprisingly, they felt let down.

In 1838, a meeting was held in Birmingham to draw up a plan of reform to help working people. It agreed on six demands. They called this 'The Charter' and its supporters became known as Chartists.

They now set about persuading Parliament to adopt their ideas. Their method was to draw up a huge **petition**, signed by thousands of people who supported the six demands. Then, it was sent to Parliament so that MPs could see just how many people did want these changes.

petition   cab   forgeries
middle class
rotten borough   Chartist

Twice they did this, in 1839 and 1842 – and twice Parliament turned it down. Each time, there were riots; each time, the government took stern measures and Chartism died down.

In 1848, there was one final petition and it was this which helped kill off the movement. The Chartists had planned a huge march across London to deliver the petition to Parliament. The government acted quickly to prevent riots. Armed troops barred the way and the petition was taken by **cabs** instead.

When Parliament received it, MPs just laughed at it. The Chartists had claimed 5 million signatures; there were actually less than 2 million, and many of those were **forgeries**. Queen Victoria alone was supposed to have signed it ten times!

Chartism had failed. There were other reasons why it ended. Life was improving for many working people. In any case, some supporters had not liked the violence; they now turned once more to trade unions.

What the Chartists wanted – and when it was achieved.

THE OLD REAL REFORMER.

"THERE WAS NO STOPPING THE SLAVE-TRADE UNTIL I MADE IT *FELONY*, AND SO IT WILL BE WITH ELECTION BRIBERY."—*Lord Brougham at Bradford.*

A A cartoon from *Punch* (1859).

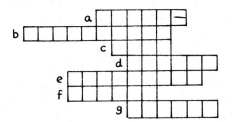

1 Copy out this grid, then fill in the answers, using the clues below.

a) Chartists wanted this sort of ballot.
b) Chartists met here in 1838.
c) The 1848 Charter was carried in these!
d) Many of these boroughs were abolished in 1832.
e) The Chartists drew up three of these.
f) Sir Charles ___ commanded troops in 1839.
g) Parliament passed a ___ Bill in 1832.

B R.G. Gammage, an ex-Chartist, wrote in 1894:

The working people met in their thousands and tens of thousands to swear devotion to the cause. It is almost impossible to imagine the excitement. The people formed into procession, making the heavens echo with the thunder of their cheers on recognizing the men who were to address them.

The banners, viewed by the red light of the glaring torches, presented a scene of awful grandeur. The death's heads on some of them grinned like ghosts. The appearance of thousands of workers, whose faces were filthy with sweat and dirt, added to the strangeness of the scene.

C Sir Charles Napier was put in charge of troops in the north in 1839. This was what he thought:

I am for a strong police, but the people should have universal suffrage, the ballot, annual Parliaments, farms for the people and education.

England has many bad laws, but is every man to arm against every law he thinks bad? No! The Chartists say they will keep the sacred month [a planned general strike]. They will do no such thing; the poor cannot do it. They must steal, and then they will be hanged by the hundreds.

They talk of their hundreds of thousands of men. Who is to move them when I am dancing round them with cavalry and pelting them with cannon shot? Poor men! How little they know of physical force!

2 a) List the six demands of the Chartists.
  b) Pick the two which you think were most important to workers. Give reasons.
  c) Which one is not in force today?
  d) Why do you think it was never made law?
3 a) Evidence A is concerned with one Chartist demand. Which one was it?
  b) What was wrong with voting in the open?
4 a) In evidence B, what would have worried the government?
  b) Is evidence C for or against Chartism? Explain your answer carefully.

13 The Golden Age of Coaching

blunderbuss
stagecoach   postboy   mail coach

Turnpike roads had brought faster travel. Unless you owned your own horse, the quickest form of transport was the stagecoach. This was a coach which travelled *by stages*, stopping at inns for fresh horses or food and drink for the passengers.

By 1800, these coaches were a great deal better than those of a century earlier. They had springs; the doors had windows in them; and narrower wheels had increased their speed.

They were too expensive for ordinary people to use, but they were fast. They were so good that the next 30 years or so are often called the Golden Age of Coaching.

One new kind of coach was the mail coach. Until the 1780s, letters had been carried by postboys. They went on horseback and wore boots stuffed with hay to keep their feet warm. It was a risky business sending a letter: postboys were often robbed and sometimes they got drunk. Above all, it was slow.

John Palmer of Bath noted that it took 38 hours to get letters from London to Bristol. Yet the stagecoach took only 17 hours. So, in 1784, he persuaded the government to let him carry out an experiment.

That year, he started the first mail coach service. Apart from letters, it also carried passengers and newspapers. Every coach had a guard, armed with a **blunderbuss** and pistols. He also carried tools to do repairs if the coach broke down; and a horn to warn toll-keepers that the coach was coming. They did not want to waste time waiting for gates to be opened.

■ BLACK   ▨ RED   ▧ MAROON   GOLD CREST

You could tell a mail coach by its colours.

The result was amazing: the time was cut to 16 hours. New mail coaches in bright maroon, black and red soon became a common sight on the roads. Only once, as far as we know, was one attacked and the guard shot dead the highwayman.

The coaching business was huge. In the 1830s, one owner was said to run 3000 stagecoaches, with 150 000 horses to pull them. Many fine coaching inns were built beside the main roads to cater for coaches and passengers.

But it was not to last. By then, a faster form of transport had been invented. It was the railway.

OPERA GLASS
CONTAINING A COMPASS
TOOTHPICK AND THERMOMETER INSIDE CANE
SNUFF
NOTES AND SKETCHES
FOR WRITING
PISTOLS
TINDER BOX
SWORD CONTAINS A BAROMETER
SHEETS AND A QUILT FOR SLEEPING

One 18th-century publication advised travellers to take all these things along on a coach journey!

A The Devonport mail coach.

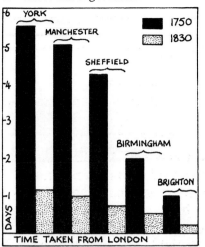

B How travel got faster:

Legend: 1750 (black), 1830 (dotted)

YORK, MANCHESTER, SHEFFIELD, BIRMINGHAM, BRIGHTON

DAYS (scale 1–6)

TIME TAKEN FROM LONDON

C From the *Leeds Mercury*, 1817:

About 6 o'clock in the morning both the coaches from Leeds to York entered the town at a full gallop. The 'True Briton', trying to pass the other coach, ran over a basket of dung which stood in the way, and was overturned.

The coach had 6 inside and 4 outside passengers but only one lady received injury. She, finding that the coach was likely to overturn, seized hold of the door, and the coach fell upon her hand. It either crushed all her fingers or bruised them so badly that they had to be amputated [cut off].

D From the *Aylesbury News*, 1837:

To get the maximum comfort possible, outside passengers should drink a tankard of good cold ale; then, rub their hands, ears and faces with snow immediately before they start. This will produce a more lasting glow than anything else.

E One traveller's journey:

Crammed full of passengers. I awake out of a sound nap with cramp in one leg and the other in a lady's box; getting out in the dark at the half-way house, in the hurry stepping into the return coach by mistake and finding yourself next morning at the very spot you had started from.

Not a breath of air – asthmatic old woman and child – unpleasant smell – shoes filled with warm water – look up and find it's the child – shut your eyes and blame the dog – pretend sleep and pinch the child – make a mistake – pinch the dog and get bit. And so it goes on.

1 a) List the ways in which the coaching age was not 'golden'.
b) Why do you think people call it 'golden'?

2 a) Draw the diagram, showing speed of travel.
b) It cost inside passengers about 1.2p per km on a coach. Write down what it cost to travel to each place on the diagram.
c) One of your group could check with the nearest coach station to find out today's cost.

3 Look at the cartoon on page 52. Write down each item on a separate line. Beside each, write down why you think it was needed.

4 a) Read the printed evidence. Write down at least two reasons why it was dangerous to travel on the outside of the coach.
b) Why *did* people travel on the outside?

5 Imagine you were the traveller in evidence E. You are so disgusted with the journey that you write a letter to the coach company to complain. Write out what you would say.

14 The Railway Age

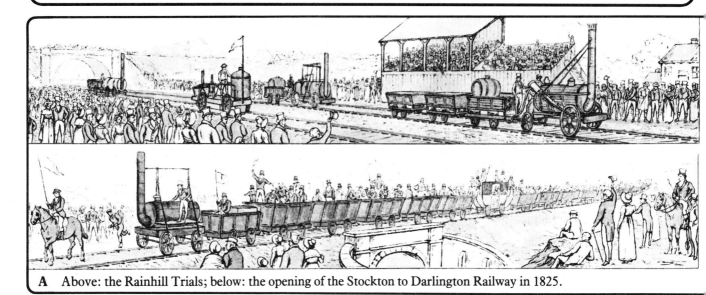

A Above: the Rainhill Trials; below: the opening of the Stockton to Darlington Railway in 1825.

cogs colliery gauge
perishable foods navigator
shanty town truck shop compensation
navvies

The first steam locomotives were at work even during the Golden Age of coaching. In 1804, Richard Trevithick ran his engine at Penydarren ironworks in Wales. It successfully pulled ten tonnes of iron for a bet.

Other engineers were quick to see the possibilities. In 1811, John Blenkinsop invented an engine with an extra wheel. It had **cogs** on it which fitted into an extra rail, giving more grip.

Then, in 1813, William Hedley built his 'Puffing Billy' to haul coal waggons at Wylam **Colliery** in Northumberland. It was so good that it was used for nearly 50 years.

Someone else grew up in the village of Wylam. He was George Stephenson, whose father looked after the pumping engine at the colliery. There were six children in the family, all living in a one-room cottage. There was no money for George to go to school.

So he started work for about 1p a day, keeping cows off the railway lines. At the age of 15, he got himself a job working the colliery engine. His pay was 60p a week – the same as his father was earning.

Engines became his life. In 1814, he built his first one, called the 'Blucher' after a famous Prussian general. It worked at 6½ km an hour. This was actually no quicker than using horses; it cost about the same, too.

But it was a start. In 1821, he was made engineer of a company which was going to build a railway from Stockton to Darlington. It was intended to use horses; Stephenson suggested using steam engines instead.

It was built mainly to carry coal. Regular passenger services had not been planned. However, the company was soon running them at a good profit, although steam engines were not used for these trains until 1833.

The railway age had begun: so had the fame of George Stephenson. In 1826, he was given a much bigger job. He was to plan and build a railway from Liverpool to Manchester. But the company was not convinced that steam engines were best.

So, in 1829, they arranged a trial at Rainhill, near Liverpool, with a prize of £500 for the best engine. The winning engine reached 46 kph. Its name? The Rocket. Its engineer? George Stephenson.

B Opening Day on the Liverpool and Manchester Railway, September 15th 1830. The directors' carriage is on the left.

C Fanny Kemble was at the opening. She described an accident which happened during the journey:

Masses of people lined the railroad, shouting and waving hats and handkerchiefs as we flew by them. I have never enjoyed anything so much as the first hour of our progress . . .

A man flew by us, calling out through a speaking-trumpet to stop the engine, for somebody in the director's coach had sustained an injury. [Soon] a hundred voices were heard exclaiming that Mr Huskisson was killed. The confusion that followed is indescribable; the urgent demands for surgical assistance created a sudden turmoil that was quite sickening.

At last we [learned] that the unfortunate man's thigh was broken. From Lady W--, who was within 3 metres of the spot where the accident happened, I had the following details, which we were spared the horror of witnessing.

The engine had stopped to take in water, and several gentlemen had jumped out to look about them. [Some] were standing talking in the middle of the road, when an engine on the other line was seen coming down upon them like lightning.

The most active sprang back into their seats, while poor Mr Huskisson, less active and bewildered, looked helplessly to right and left and was instantly [thrown down] by the fatal machine. It passed over his leg, smashing and mangling it in the most horrible way. (Lady W-- said she distinctly heard the crushing of the bone.) So terrible was the effect that, [apart from] that ghastly 'crushing' and poor Mrs Huskisson's piercing shriek, not a sound was heard or a word uttered among the spectators nearby.

1   Each of these dates is important in railway history:
    1830; 1813; 1804; 1821; 1829; 1811; 1825; 1826; 1814.
    Write each date on a separate line, in chronological order. Beside each date, write what happened in that year.

2   Look carefully at evidence A.
    a) What did most passengers travel in for the opening of the Stockton-Darlington line?
    b) Who do you think travelled in the coach?
    c) Why do you think there is a horseman carrying a flag?

d) Do you think these drawings are reliable? Give reasons for your answer.

3   a) Look at evidence B. Why do you think important people were asked to be present?
    b) Which of the following words describe Fanny Kemble's *real* feelings about the accident:
        shocked; horrified; fascinated; embarrassed; amused; sickened; excited; disgusted?
    Give reasons for your choices.
    c) What do you think the directors felt about the accident?

Railway Development

The Liverpool and Manchester Railway was an immediate success. It ran the first regular passenger service and was soon carrying 1200 passengers a day. Travelling by train became all the rage.

There was no shortage of people who wanted to build railways, either. Up and down the country, companies were being formed to build new lines.

It worked in the same way as building the canals. A group of people raised the money, then they asked Parliament for permission to build their line. It was a costly business, but there were good profits to be made.

Most of these lines were small, local ones, but there were exceptions. In 1838, George Stephenson's son, Robert, finished work on the London to Birmingham Railway.

In 1841, Isambard Kingdom Brunel completed his Great Western Railway, from London to Bristol. It used a 7 feet (213 cms) **gauge**, instead of the 4ft 8½ ins (143 cms) used by Stephenson. Brunel said it allowed faster and more comfortable trains.

The 1840s saw many changes which helped to improve the railways. At the same time, cheaper fares made rail travel more popular.

1844 RAILWAY ACT
EVERY COMPANY HAD TO RUN AT LEAST ONE TRAIN A DAY IN EACH DIRECTION AT A CHEAP RATE OF 1d (0·4p) A MILE, STOPPING AT ALL STATIONS.

1846 STANDARD GAUGE CHOSEN
PARLIAMENT DECIDED THAT ALL NEW RAILWAYS MUST BE BUILT TO THE SAME GAUGE OF 4'8½".

Yet some people complained. Some towns refused to have a railway station in the town at all. Landowners were sometimes bitterly opposed to new lines. Even George Stephenson had to do some surveying at night to be safe!

Some of the complaints were understandable. Canal companies, stagecoach owners and turnpike trusts had most to lose. But some other objections were pretty ridiculous:

Objections to railways.

However, none of this stopped the spread of the railways. By 1850, the country had over 10 600 km of track. Building did not really slow down until the 1880s. The Great Central main line was not finished until 1899.

The results were enormous. Rail travel was half the cost of going by stagecoach – and so much faster. Letters and newspapers could also be delivered much more quickly. Of course, the building industry benefited as there was such a demand for materials to build the lines.

Perhaps the greatest effect was on ordinary people. They could look for work more easily, and live further from it. Cheap travel meant they could get around more. People who had never seen the seaside before could now take a day trip.

There was another bonus for town-dwellers. **Perishable foods** were cheaper and fresher than ever before. Milk and vegetables could be brought from much further away. So could fish. Before the railway came, towns such as West Bromwich did not have a single fish shop. Many people had the railways to thank for their fish and chips!

A

B

C

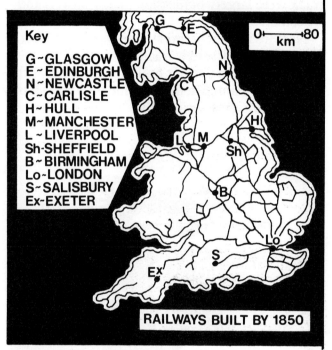

D   Railways by 1850.

A, B and **C**   Three classes of rail travel in 1847.

1   Explain how each of these helped railway development:
(a) Robert Stephenson; (b) I. K. Brunel;
(c) The 1844 Railway Act; (d) the Standard Gauge Act.

2   Look carefully at the cartoon on page 56.
a) Which objection do you think would most concern (i) an MP; (ii) a landowner?
b) Pick any three of the complaints and write down how you would persuade someone that they were nothing to worry about.

3   a) From what you read on page 56, which groups of people benefited from the railways?
b) Apart from those mentioned, who else do you think gained from rail transport?

4   Look at evidence A, B and C.
a) Write down which class of travel is shown in each picture (first, second or third).
b) What comforts does the first class have that the third class does not have?

5   a) Draw the map of railway development.
b) *Either* find out which line was nearest to where you live *or* find out when your local line was built.

Navvies

The railways also created jobs, thousands of them. At one time, one out of every 100 workers worked for the railways. They included the people who built them. These were the navvies, which is short for **navigators**.

By 1847, there was a vast army of 250 000 navvies. Many of these men came from the north or Scotland; others came from Ireland, especially when times were hard.

Why were there so many? Because there was none of the machinery we have today. Most of the work was done by hand. The tunnels, bridges and track were largely built using picks, shovels and wheelbarrows.

Navvies lived wherever a line was being built. They followed the new track across the countryside. On a major building job, such as the Woodhead Tunnel in the Pennines, a whole **shanty town** of huts grew up nearby.

Romantic idea of a navvy. In fact, navvy costume varied from one region to another and he rarely looked like this.

A typical hut housed about 20 navvies. They slept two to a bed, for 1½p each a night. Those who could not afford that paid ⅕p to sleep on the floor. At one end of the room was a huge pot for cooking. Each navvy had his own meal, cooked in a net which dangled in the pot. Navvies ate and drank well. They needed to: the work was tough.

Perhaps shovelling earth and rocks sounds a pretty straightforward job, but it does require strength. A good navvy could shift about 20 tonnes of earth a day. New workers couldn't cope with a whole day of it. They were exhausted by mid-afternoon!

But navvies were well paid for the time. A typical wage was 25p a day, although they might have to wait two months for pay day. The railway company often built an alehouse, where pay was handed out.

The company usually had its own shop, too, called a **truck shop**. It was handy for the navvies to shop at it, but goods were usually overpriced.

After pay day, work might stop for days on end, while the navvies went on a drinking spree. They called it 'going on a randy'. It was a warning to local folk to lock their doors and keep out of the way. When the navvies' pay was spent, they went back to work again.

The navvies spent about £620 on drink for every kilometre of track they built.

The navvies worked hard as well as played hard. The death rate was high. Tunnels sometimes flooded or caved in; men were careless with dynamite; work was done in a hurry. Time cost money – but navvies could always be replaced. Employers paid little **compensation** for injuries. A man's widow might get £5, if she was lucky.

The navvies knew the risks and there was little sympathy for those injured. One lad whose foot was crushed was told, 'Crying'll do you no good. You'd better have it cut off above the knee.'

But the employers knew the value of their workers. In later years, many British navvies built railways overseas. In France, they were paid at least twice what the others earned. They worked that much harder.

A If the navvies didn't go to church, the church came to them!

B Daily pay on the Settle to Carlisle line, 1869:

Labourers 20p
Carpenters 27½p
Smiths 27½p
Masons 30p
Miners 32½p

C A Wiltshire woman described early married life in the 1840s:

'Twas wintertime coming, and they was working nothing but muck. Charley was tipping then, like he is here; and 'tis dreadful hard to get the stuff out of the wagons when 'tis streaming wet atop and all stodge under. Then, you see, he was standing in his boots all day long; and twice when he draw'd out his foot, the sole of his boot was left in the dirt; new ones, too, for he had a new pair of 75p boots every week. So he cudn't stand that long.

One Saturday night he took out his back money and said us wid tramp for Yorkshire; for he'd a work'd there and 'twas all rock, and beautiful for tunnels. I didn' know where Yorkshire was; I hadn' never been 32 kilometres nowhere. I wasn' but just seventeen year old, and I didn' like for to go. 'Twas then us began for to quarley so.

He took his kit, and I had my pillow strapped to my back; and off us sot, jawing all along. Us walked 48 km a day, dead on end. It never stopped raining, and I hadn't a dry thread on me night or day, for us slept in such mis'rable holes of places, I was afeard my clothes 'ud be stole if I took 'em off.

Us comed to Leeds. Well, if this is Yorkshire, us had better a stopped where us was, dirt and all. And what a lingo they talk! I cudn' for the life of me understand 'em; and I were glad that Charley cudn' git work he liked there. So us had three days' more tramp – just 160 km – to a tunnel.

1 Write one sentence about each of these: navvies; shanty town; truck shop.
2 Think of the different jobs a navvy might do. Each job carried risks. Write down the jobs and the dangers they involved. For instance, one job was to blast away rock, using dynamite. The danger was that there could be an explosion.
3 a) Look at the picture of a navvy on page 58.
   b) He is carrying various objects. Name as many of them as possible and explain why he needed them.
   c) Which object would you not expect a real navvy to carry – and why?
4 Read evidence B. Why do you think some navvies were paid more than others?
5 Read evidence C and work out what it says! Imagine you were the navvy's wife, writing home to your parents. Tell them about what you're doing and what you dislike about the navvy way of life.

Although industry had grown fast, the government had left the owners to run their factories and mines as they wished. Many people thought that what was good for industry had to be good for Britain.

We call this policy *laissez-faire*. It means 'leave alone'. The result was misery for thousands of workers. Children who worked in the small, older mills suffered the most.

Of course, some factory-owners were good employers and looked after their workers. But there were plenty of others who looked upon workers as not much better than machines. One mill in Salford was actually nicknamed the 'Cripple Factory'.

As time passed, however, many people, including some MPs, began to think it was wrong to ignore what was happening. After all, the slave trade had been banned in 1807. Yet, in Britain itself, children of five and six were working in conditions which made them little better than slaves.

In fact, Parliament had *tried* to improve things slightly. In 1802 and 1819, two Factory Acts had been passed. The first of these tried to improve the lives of factory apprentices:

laissez-faire   disgraced

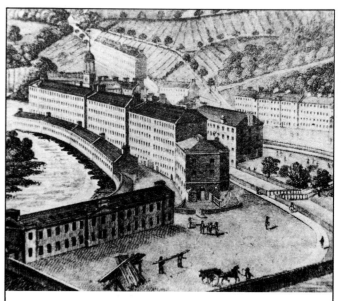

The factory town at New Lanark in 1820.

The most famous mill-owner who *did* care for his workers was Robert Owen, who owned a mill at New Lanark in Scotland. He believed that factory-owners could make good profits by *reducing* workers' hours and treating them well.

He built them good houses and a school. Children aged three upwards could go to the school until they started working in the factory at the age of ten. These ideas worked. Owen still made a good profit and his workers were healthy and worked hard.

But few owners followed his example. Owen wanted to change society and give workers a greater share in the new wealth. Many mill-owners were suspicious of him because of this.

In later life, many of his ideas failed badly. One of them was the Grand National Consolidated Trades Union, which he had set up. It was this union which encouraged the farm labourers of Tolpuddle.

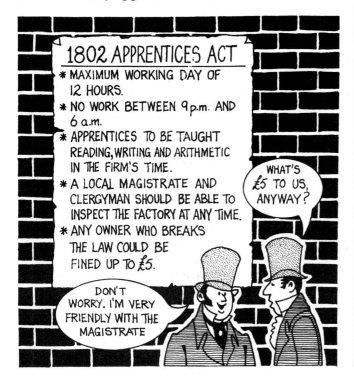

1802 APPRENTICES ACT
* MAXIMUM WORKING DAY OF 12 HOURS.
* NO WORK BETWEEN 9 p.m. AND 6 a.m.
* APPRENTICES TO BE TAUGHT READING, WRITING AND ARITHMETIC IN THE FIRM'S TIME.
* A LOCAL MAGISTRATE AND CLERGYMAN SHOULD BE ABLE TO INSPECT THE FACTORY AT ANY TIME.
* ANY OWNER WHO BREAKS THE LAW COULD BE FINED UP TO £5.

WHAT'S £5 TO US, ANYWAY?

DON'T WORRY. I'M VERY FRIENDLY WITH THE MAGISTRATE

In the 1830s, a number of leading figures began to campaign for a ten-hour working day. That sounds long to us today, but remember that many young children were working up to 16 hours a day at the time.

The campaigners were led by Richard Oastler, a land agent, Michael Sadler, an MP, and a mill-owner named John Fielden. They gathered evidence to prove just how bad things were. Many factory-owners disagreed with them, of course, but the public was horrified.

In 1832, Parliament held an enquiry. Groups of MPs questioned factory-owners and workers. Their report was quite clear that:
* Children were overworked.
* Their health suffered as a result.
* They could not get an education or – if they could – they were too tired to benefit from it.

Parliament's action is explained in this picture:

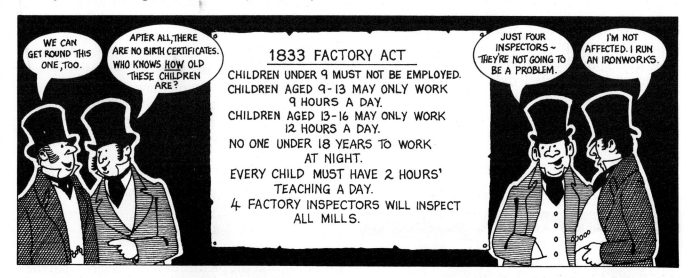

A Women in the dress-making trade were some of the poorest paid. Because they worked at home, they were not helped by any of these Acts of Parliament.

B Josiah Wedgwood employed 13 children under 10 years and another 103, aged 10–18, in 1816. He told Parliament:

The hours of work for dippers in my factory are from 8 or 9 o'clock in the morning, to about 5 in the afternoon; the hours for other persons are from half past 6 in the morning to 6 in the evening, with half an hour for breakfast and an hour for dinner. But we have a custom [sometimes] of working extra hours, to 9 o'clock in the evening.

The children work the same time. The wages of the children are paid, I believe in all cases, to the parents. Too often, these wages are employed by the parents not in giving the children improved clothing and food but in [buying] liquor for themselves.

I have a strong opinion that, from all I know of factories in general, and certainly of my own, we had better be left alone.

The reformers were disappointed. They wanted everyone to work a ten-hour day at the longest. In any case, the Act only helped children working in textile mills. It said nothing about those in coal-mines – or many other industries where conditions were dreadful.

The reformers found it was a slow business. The employers argued every step of the way. Even when they lost, some of them still managed to think of a way to avoid keeping to the new laws.

The new laws, and what they said, are shown on the right. None of these Acts much limited men's hours. Many people felt that, if a man wanted to work himself to death, that was up to him.

The ten-hour day itself did not come about until 1874, but Parliament's attitude was slowly changing. The 19th century had seen great changes in people's working lives; most of them had been for the better.

By 1900, Parliament was beginning to accept that it had a duty to look after *all* the people of the country. Today, no one would doubt that.

1842 Mines Act	No women or children under ten to work down a mine. Inspectors appointed.
1844 Factory Act	Women to work 12-hour day at a maximum. Machinery to be fenced in for safety.
1847 Ten Hour Act	Ten-hour day for all women and young people under 18. Maximum 58 hours a week.
1850 Factory Act	Machinery only to operate between 6 a.m. and 6 p.m. Increased the hours for women and children to 10½ per day.
1867 Factory Extensions Act	Factory laws now covered all industries which employed more than 50 workers.
1895 Factory Act	Children under 13 to work only a 30-hour week.

The 1842 Mines Act left about 2000 women unemployed. Some were so desperate for money that they disguised themselves as men to get back into the mines.

C A witness in 1832 said:

On one occasion I was with a West India slave master and three Bradford spinners. They compared the two systems and the spinners were silent when the slave owner said:

'I have always thought myself disgraced [ashamed] by being the owner of black slaves. But we in the West Indies never thought it was possible for any human being to be so cruel as to require a child of nine years old to work twelve and a half hours a day.'

1 a) Look at the picture of New Lanark. List the ways in which living here should be healthier than in the towns described on pages 30 to 35.
b) In your own words, explain why other owners did not follow Owen's example.

2 Which pictures on pages 60 – 62 do you think are evidence? Give reasons for your choices.

3 a) Read carefully the details of the 1802 Act on page 60. Write down as many reasons as possible why this Act would not be a complete success.
b) Now, do the same for the 1833 Act on page 61.

4 a) Read evidence B on page 61. Think of one improvement which Mr Wedgwood could make, even if he goes on employing children.
b) Now, write a letter to Mr Wedgwood, trying to persuade him not to employ children at all.
c) Read evidence C opposite. Do you agree or disagree with the speaker? Give reasons.

5 a) Look carefully at the picture at the bottom of page 61. Write down what you can see at numbers 1 to 4.
b) What is figure 5 doing?
c) What do you think the artist felt about the dress-making trade?

Revision

1 The square below contains the names of various people who have been mentioned in the last 30 pages. They run in sequence, starting in the top left corner. The first name – STEPHENSON – is shown by a line. Write each name down and explain why each person is famous.

```
S   T   E   P   A   R   A   D
N   O   S   H   L   K   H   W
H   E   N   E   C   S   C   I
N   D   L   E   Y   O   N   C
E   S   E   C   R   O   F   K
D   S   L   E   B   R   R   W
L   F   E   L   L   U   E   I
E   I   V   O   E   N   B   L
```

2 There are always at least two ways of looking at any event. Here are eight headlines which could have appeared in 19th century newspapers. They are about four events.
a) Pair up the headlines so that you have one for and one against each event.
b) Write down the names of the four events.
c) Then, for each event, write down a headline which is *not* biased.
d) Choose any one of them and write your own *unbiased* news story about it.
(1) 1830: Wonderful Opening Of New Railway
(2) Transportation For Farm Labourers: Good Riddance To Bad Rubbish!
(3) Slave Owners Ruined By Government Decision
(4) Court's Unfair Decision: Six Martyrs Found Guilty
(5) Government Free Poor Infants From Slavery Underground
(6) Slaves Go Free – Owners Get Finally Beaten
(7) MP Dies Horribly And People Demand: Ban The Ugly Steam Monsters
(8) Country Faces Huge Debts Now Mines Act Is Passed

3 Where are they?
Draw the grid below in your book, using a pencil and ruler. Next, look at what the people underneath are saying. Your job is to work out where each speaker is. For example, if you think speaker 1 is at Tolpuddle, put a tick beside Tolpuddle in column 1.

	1	2	3	4	5	6
Cotton Mill						
Village after Enclosure						
Prison						
On a stagecoach						
At a Luddite riot						
Rainhill Trials						
Ironworks						
Coal-mine						
Tolpuddle						

16   Scenes from Family Life

Empire   attic   governess

The Working Class

Family life hardly existed for many workers during the Industrial Revolution. Everyone in the family worked long hours and came home exhausted. The children were sometimes carried home asleep.

Sunday was their one day off but many people just sat around. They had little money to pay for amusements; many were just too tired to amuse themselves.

So a housewife found little time for keeping the house clean. Getting fresh water often meant a long walk, so the same water was used over and over again. In any case, the water itself was usually filthy.

Anyway, there was not much to keep clean. Most poor families had the minimum of furniture; some families did not even own a bed. They just put straw on the floor. Their few belongings were kept in boxes.

They did not need a wardrobe because few poor people had a change of clothes. They did their washing on Sunday and hoped it would be dry, ready for work on Monday. If not, they wore it damp.

Babies were given Godfrey's Cordial to keep them quiet. It was a mixture of opium and treacle!

A   A widow with four children in Bradford, 1849:

There are two rooms here and the rent is 10p. I know it's too much for the like of me to pay; but think of the children. Well, sir, the parish are very good to me, and give me 15p a week – 10p for the rent and 5p for coals – and we live and clothe ourselves on the other 40p. [She earns 30p; her young son earns 10p a week.]

We live chiefly on bread. I get a stone and a half [9.5 kilos] of flour every week, and I bake it on Sundays. Then we have a little tea and coffee, and sometimes we have a little offal meat, because it's cheap. A good gentleman gave me the furniture I have, and the bed in the other room. It cost altogether 75p. Everybody has been very kind to me and neighbours come in often to look after the children when I'm at work.

Their homes were often damp, too – and cold, dark and dirty. Edwin Chadwick was probably right when he said that most factories were better than people's homes. There was a high death-rate among those children who were too young to go to work.

Couples got married young and had large families. Ten children was not unusual. After all, children were a source of income. But few parents knew much about bringing them up: they had not been to school and had started work too young to have time to learn.

The homes of farm workers were little better. The air might be fresher; the houses were less crammed together; however, inside, the signs of poverty were much the same.

Such a lot of children died young that death was a common feature of everyday life. If someone did die, there was nowhere to put the body until the funeral. It just stayed in the room and life went on around it. Children's bodies were often laid out on the table.

By 1900, things were getting better. Housing had improved; so had living conditions. But there was still great poverty. Out of every 100 babies, 15 died before the age of one. Over one-third of the population did not earn enough to live on. It was left to the 20th century to try to solve that problem.

B A typical family day in Manchester, 1832:

5.00 a.m.   Wake up
6.00 a.m   Begin work at the mill
8.00 a.m.   Breakfast (tea and bread or porridge)
8.30 a.m   Work begins again
12 noon   Dinner (boiled potatoes in melted lard or butter; perhaps, a little fried bacon)
1.00 p.m.   Return to the mill
7.00 p.m.   End of day's work followed by supper (tea and bread)

D Sunday at home in 1873:

C The Crick family's budget: Expenditure (in pence)

Bread	45
Potatoes	5
Rent	6
Tea	0.8
Sugar	1.45
Soap	1.25
Blue	0.2
Thread, etc	0.8
Candles	1.25
Salt	0.2
Coal and wood	3.75
Butter	1.8
Cheese	1.25
Total expenditure	68.75

E 'The Home of the Rick-burner' – a cartoon from 1844.

1 Which of the five families in the evidence do you think is poorest? Give reasons.

2 Answer each question in a complete sentence:
  a) Why was house-cleaning a difficult job?
  b) Why did people sometimes wear damp clothes?
  c) Why did many mothers know little about bringing up children?
  d) Why do you think Godfrey's Cordial was dangerous?

3 Look at evidence D and E. For *each* room write down the signs of poverty you can see.

4 Look carefully at evidence C.
  a) What common items do they not buy?
  b) Why don't they buy them?
  c) From their purchases, work out a rough plan for their meals for a *week*.
  d) What do you notice about the meals you have planned?

5 How does the budget of the woman in evidence A differ from that in evidence C?

6 What impression do you get of the woman in evidence A? Write down what you think she is like.

The Middle Class

Yet all these poor people lived in a country which was rich. In the middle of the 19th century, their country owned a large **Empire**. And that Empire went on growing throughout the rest of the century. At home and abroad, there were plenty of customers for British products.

As a result, some people were becoming much better off. They included the factory-owners and mine-owners; merchants and businessmen; and professional people, such as lawyers. These people belonged to the middle classes, and many of them were growing rich.

It showed in the way they lived. They could afford big homes in which they brought up large families. These houses were being built with **attics** to be used as servants' rooms. The servants had low wages, so there were many of them to do all the work around the house.

Inside, there were many signs of luxury, such as gas lighting. (Some would soon have gas cookers, too.) Thick carpets covered the floors and heavy curtains hung at the windows. The sitting room was filled with heavy, carved furniture with leather seats. Often, there was a piano or organ in one corner.

There might even be photographs on the wall. Photography was a new invention which was quickly catching on. Rich parents liked to have photographs of their families to put in albums or show off to their friends. Queen Victoria was as keen as anyone.

Middle-class wives did not work for a living. They did not need to. In any case, middle-class husbands frowned on their wives having jobs. They thought that a woman's place was in the home. A man's word was law to his family.

The family day began with prayers before breakfast. Everyone, including the servants, would join in. At other meals, some servants were present to serve the food.

A   A Victorian family at home in 1858.

Meal-times were usually quiet. Parents were very strict about their children's manners. In many families, children only joined in the conversation if an adult spoke to them.

The boys would go away to public school when they were old enough; the girls stayed at home and were taught by a governess. This was one of the few ways an unmarried middle-class woman could earn a living. Many **governesses** led miserable lives, for just 50p a week in pay.

The middle classes were proud of their homes. They were confident about the future. After all, Britain was called the 'Workshop of the World'. In 1851, Prince Albert, the Queen's husband, was planning an exhibition to prove it.

JUST SOME OF THE SERVANTS' JOBS...				
5·30 a.m.	9·30 a.m.	AFTER LUNCH	AFTERNOON	...AND A YEAR'S EARNINGS IN THE 1850's:
LIGHTING THE FIRE	EMPTYING BASINS FROM BEDROOMS	WASHING UP WITH SODA	CLEANING WINDOWS WITH PARAFFIN	HOUSEMAID £12 COOK £15 GOVERNESS £21

Servants' pay – and what they did to earn it.

B A Victorian sitting-room.

C Yearly income of different classes in 1867:

Upper class	Over £5000
Upper middle class	£1000–£5000
Middle class	£300–£1000
Lower middle class	£100–£300
Labouring class	Mainly below £100

D Mrs Beeton gave advice on how many servants to have according to family income:

About £1000 a year: Cook, housemaid, and perhaps a man-servant.
From £750 to £500 a year: Cook, housemaid.
About £300 a year: General servant.
About £200 a year: Young girl for rough work.

1 Copy out and complete this paragraph:
    The middle classes included _____ and _____ owners, _____, _____ and professional people. They could afford _____ houses and employed _____ to do the housework. Their sons were educated at _____ schools, while their daughters were taught by _____.

2 a) Look at evidence A. How do you know that this family is well-off? (You should note at least five clues.)
    b) What are they doing in the picture?
    c) List the main differences between this room and evidence D on page 65.

3 What are the main differences between evidence B and your living room?

4 a) Give *two* reasons why middle-class families wanted servants.
    b) Why did so many people become servants if they were poorly paid? Were there any advantages in the job?

5 If you had been an early photographer, what would you have photographed to show later generations what life was like then? Write down your choices and explain how you decided.

17   The Great Exhibition   1851

4500 tons of iron

293 655 panes of glass

Cost £335 742

Over 100 000 exhibits

The 1851 Exhibition in Hyde Park, London, was the first **international** exhibition. Everything about it was on the grand scale. That included the building itself.

It was designed by a gardener called Joseph Paxton, who was famous for designing greenhouses. The building he planned was rather like a huge greenhouse itself.

It was made of glass and metal, with a great curved roof so that trees growing on the site did not have to be cut down. There was so much glass that people called it the Crystal Palace. Inside was a stunning display of the very latest and best goods you could find anywhere.

Queen Victoria was as excited as anyone. She went twice even before the official opening day to watch her husband's idea take shape. Like everyone else, she thought the building was marvellous. 'One of the wonders of the world,' she called it.

The Exhibition was opened by the Queen on May 1st 1851. That same day, 2500 people visited

it – and people went on going right up until it closed on October 11th. In all, over 6 million people paid to go round.

Even the profit was on a big scale. It made over £180 000, a huge sum for those days. It was even more remarkable considering that, on most days, it only cost 5p to get in. The price was kept low to encourage working class families to have a day out at the Exhibition.

Hundreds of special trains brought them to the capital. Dozens of horse-drawn buses took them across the city. They even put seats on top for the first time to cope with all the extra passengers.

Britain was a great nation and it was enjoying showing off. Indeed, people did not want it to end. On the last day, people were in tears as the **National Anthem** was played.

People could not bear to lose the building, either, so they took it to pieces and moved it to South London. It stayed there until 1936 when a fire completely destroyed it.

A The Great Exhibition on Opening Day, 1851 (left).

B A cartoon of 1850, showing those who made clothes (right).

THE WONDER OF 1851!

FROM YORK
TO LONDON AND BACK FOR A CROWN.

THE MIDLAND RAILWAY COMPANY
Will continue to run

TWO TRAINS DAILY
(Excepted Sunday, when only one Train is available)

FOR THE GREAT EXHIBITION,
UNTIL SATURDAY, OCTOBER 11.

Without any Advance of Payment

RETURN SPECIAL TRAINS leave the Euston Station on MONDAYS, TUESDAYS, THURSDAYS, & SATURDAYS at 11 a.m., on WEDNESDAYS and FRIDAYS at 1 p.m., and EVERY NIGHT (Sundays excepted) at 9 p.m.

First and Second Class Tickets are available for returning any day (except Sunday) up to and including Monday, Oct. 20. Third Class Tickets issued before the 6th instant are available for 14 days, and all issued after the 6th are returnable any day up to Monday the 20th.

The Trains leave York at 9-40 a.m. every day except Sunday, and also every day, including Sunday, at 7-20 p.m.

Fares to London and Back :—

1st Class 15s. 2nd, 10s, 3rd, 5s.
The Midland is the only Company that runs Trains Daily at these Fares.
Ask for Midland Tickets !

Children above 3 and under 12 years of age, Half-price. Luggage allowed—112 lbs. to First Class, 100 lbs. to Second, and 56 lbs. to Third Class Passengers.

APPROVED LODGINGS, of all classes, are provided in London for Passengers by Midland Trains. The Agents will give Tickets of reference on application, without charge, and an Office is opened in London, at DONALD's WATERLOO DINING ROOMS, 14, Seymour-street, near Euston Station, where an agent is in regular attendance to conduct parties who go up unprepared with Lodgings.

The Managers have much pleasure in stating that the immense numbers who have travelled under their arrangements have been conducted in perfect safety—indeed in the history of the Midland Lines, *no accident, attended with personal injury, has ever happened to an Excursion Train.* In conducting the extraordinary traffic of this Great Occasion the first object is to ensure *safety,* and that object has hitherto been most happily achieved.

With the fullest confidence, inspired by past success, the Conductors have pleasure in urging those who have not yet visited the Exhibition, to avail themselves of the present facilities, and to improve the opportunity which will close on the 11th of October.

All communications respecting the Trains to be addressed to the Managers, for the Company,

John Cuttle & John Calverley, Wakefield;
Thomas Cook, Leicester.

October 2nd, 1851.

T. COOK, PRINTER, 28, GRANBY-STREET, LEICESTER.

C Railway poster advertising a cheap excursion trip.

The Great Exhibition marked the high point of Britain's industrial progress, and its effects were felt for years afterwards. Just one of the machines on show was one which made buttons.

It was quick; it was cheap. And it meant the end of one of the few domestic industries left. In Dorset, there was a big home button-making industry; by 1900, it had practically stopped.

1   This word search contains the names of just a few of the exhibits in 1851. Write down all those you can find.

```
C H I N A H O E
A S S A L G R G
R X N U S O F A
P N O V H T S I
E I T C O A L R
T P T P A P E R
E A U E F A S A
W M B W T R A C
```

2   What contribution did these people make to the Exhibition: (a) Joseph Paxton; (b) Prince Albert; (c) Queen Victoria?

3   a) Look carefully at evidence B. Write down what it says on the four glass jars.
b) How did *each* of these people contribute to the Exhibition?
c) What idea is the cartoonist trying to get over?
d) Guess why the old man is still working. (Clue: he wouldn't have to work, if he lived today.)

4   a) How does evidence C encourage people to go to visit the Exhibition?
b) Design your own poster to advertise it. Use some of the details on these two pages to make it as realistic as possible.

POOR BOX

Royal Commission
poor rate   Speenhamland system
orphan   union   'Workhouse Test'

In 1700, many rich people believed that, if you were poor, it was your own fault. Poor people were wicked. So the best way to deal with the poor was to punish them.

Each parish collected a tax called the poor rate. This money was used to support the paupers. Some parishes built workhouses where paupers had to live and work for a living. Many other parishes found it was easier just to give the poor money to buy food and leave them to live wherever they could.

In the late 18th century, bread prices shot up and the number of poor people, especially farm workers, increased. In 1795, Berkshire magistrates met at the village of Speen to fix farm workers' wages.

Instead of increasing these wages, they worked out a system which would give the poor extra money from the poor rate. This became known as the Speenhamland system and it quickly caught on in south and east England. For nearly 40 years, wages stayed down and the poor rate rose. This diagram shows why:

As time passed, many people felt that the system was actually encouraging people not to work. In any case, it was very expensive. By 1832, the

THE POOR PICKING THE BONES TO LIVE

government was concerned enough to set up a **Royal Commission** to look into the subject.

At that time, each parish was looking after all kinds of paupers:
* orphans (children without parents)
* the old and the sick
* able-bodied (fit) adults without a job

The Commission decided that it was the last group which needed dealing with. Their view was that many could find work if they tried. So the Commission's solution was to make a pauper's life so miserable that they would want to go out and get a job.

In 1834, the government passed the Poor Law Amendment Act. Parishes were to join together to form Unions, and each Union would have its own workhouse. Life in the workhouse would be made worse than the poorest life outside. Any able-bodied person who wanted help would have to live in the workhouse to receive it.

This was called the 'workhouse test'. It was to test how badly you needed help. If you were willing to enter a workhouse, it was clear proof of just how desperate you were.

People really came to fear the workhouse, but it did not solve the problem of paupers. Even in 1900, about one-third of the population in the towns were living below the poverty line. The workhouse simply made sure that the poorest of all lived the most miserable of lives.

THE COMMISSION OF INQUIRY DISCUSSING THE SUBJECT OVER
A GOOD DINNER.

A Workers at Andover Workhouse spent 8 hours a day crushing bones. In 1845, it was discovered that they were so hungry that some people were gnawing them. These two drawings were published at the time.

B Samuel Green, aged 61, said:

I was employed in the workhouse at bone-breaking the best part of my time. I have seen a great many marrow bones brought in. We looked out for the fresh bones; we used to tell the fresh bones by the look of them, and then we used to be like a parcel of dogs after them.

I have picked a sheep's head, a mutton bone and a beef bone, when they were fresh and good; sometimes I have had one that was stale and stunk, and I eat it even then because I was hungered, I suppose.

You see, we only had bread and gruel for breakfast and, as there was no bread allowed on meat days for dinner, we saved our bread from breakfast. Then, we were hungry before dinner-time.

The allowance of potatoes at dinner on meat days is half a pound [226 grammes], but we used to get nearly a pound, seven or eight middling sized potatoes. The food we got in the workhouse was very good; I could not wish better; all I wanted was a little more. No man has occasion to find fault with the bread. The cheese was very good cheese.

I have seen a man named Reeves eat horse flesh off the bones which had been brought from Squire Smith's; I have seen him do it often. I told him it was horse flesh, but he did not care; it went down sweet as a nut.

I once saw Eaton take up a horse's leg, and take the hair off it, and eat the flesh. The leg was not cooked. Eaton is weak in his intellect, and I don't think he has got any taste, or smell either.

STOCKTON UNION.
Dietary for able-bodied Men and Women.

		BREAKFAST.		DINNER.				SUPPER.	
		Bread.	Boiled Milk with Oatmeal.	Cooked Meat.	Potatoes.	Suet Pudding.	Soup or Rice Milk.	Bread.	Boiled Milk with Oatmeal or Broth.
		Oz.	Pints.	Oz.	lbs.	Oz.	Pints.	Oz.	Pints.
Sunday	Men	6	1½	....	....	14	....	6	1½
	Women	6	1½	....	....	14	....	6	1½
Monday	Men	6	1½	5	½		....	6	1½
	Women	6	1½	5	½		....	6	1½
Tuesday	Men	6	1½	....	....		1½	6	1½
	Women	6	1½	....	....		1½	6	1½
Wednesday	Men	6	1½	....	....	14	....	6	1½
	Women	6	1½	....	....	14	....	6	1½
Thursday	Men	6	1½	....	....		1½	6	1½
	Women	6	1½	....	....		1½	6	1½
Friday	Men	6	1½	5	½		....	6	1½
	Women	6	1½	5	½		....	6	1½
Saturday	Men	6	1½	....	....		1½	6	1½
	Women	6	1½	....	....		1½	6	1½

Old People above 60 years of age, may be allowed Tea, Coffee, Butter, and Sugar, (not exceeding 1 oz. of Tea, 2 oz. of Coffee, 3½ oz. of Butter, and 4 oz. of Sugar, per week each) in lieu of Gruel to Breakfast. Greens, occasionally, in lieu of Potatoes.

4 oz. of Bread to Soup and Rice Milk Dinners, to each Person.

Children under 9 years of age dieted at discretion. Sick dieted as ordered by the Medical Officer.

C A workhouse diet in about 1850.

1 Explain each of these words:
   workhouse; Union; poor rate; pauper; orphan; 'workhouse test'.
2 Explain why each of these dates was important:
   1795; 1832; 1834.
Look at all the evidence before answering the rest of the questions.
3 a) What happened at Andover workhouse?
   b) Why do you think people were shocked?
   c) Why do you think the newspaper printed the two cartoons (evidence A) side by side?
   d) What did Samuel Green think was (i) good and (ii) bad about the workhouse food?
   e) Do you believe him? Give reasons.
4 a) Look at evidence C. What was the main food?
   b) What was missing from this diet?

19   Climbing Boys . . .

Orphans did not stay in workhouses for very long. They were usually made apprentices at an early age. None suffered more than the climbing boys.

These were young children who worked for chimney sweeps. Their job was to climb inside chimneys and scrape the **soot** from the walls.

The children were supposed to be learning their trade: they were really the sweep's assistants. But some master sweeps treated them as little better than slaves.

Owners usually wanted their chimneys cleaned in the early morning . There were few people around at that time to see how it was done. In any case, people wanted clean chimneys. *How* they were cleaned really did not bother them.

If the chimneys had been built straight and wide, they could easily have been brushed clean. But many chimneys were crooked and narrow. Some only measured 23 centimetres square. So children climbed inside to clean them.

Many house-holders insisted on using children even in wider chimneys, long after machines had been invented. They were afraid of soot damaging their carpets.

Boys were sometimes so tired that their master had to force them to go to work. If the child hesitated at the bottom of the chimney, his master stuck pins in his feet. Or lit a fire to force the child to keep climbing.

Parliament passed law after law to get things changed, but climbing boys went on being used until 1875:

* 1788: No apprentice sweeps under 8 years old
* 1834: No child under 10 to be employed
* 1840: No person under 21 to sweep chimneys
  (Fine of £10 for anyone breaking this law)

But boys went on being used until:
* 1875: Sweeps to be **licensed**. Licences only given to sweeps not using climbing boys

The 1875 Act was passed mainly through the efforts of Lord Shaftesbury, who spent much of his life trying to help poor children. When he died in 1885, the public collected money for a **memorial** in London. It still stands in the middle of Piccadilly Circus today.

soot   licensed   memorial
illegitimate

A   A master sweep described what boys went through (1863):

No one knows the cruelty which a boy has to undergo in learning. The flesh must be hardened. This is done by rubbing it, chiefly on the elbows and knees with the strongest brine, close by a hot fire. You must stand over them with a cane, or coax them with a halfpenny, if they will stand a few more rubs.

At first they come back from their work with their arms and knees streaming with blood, and the knees looking as if the caps had been pulled off. Then they must be rubbed with brine again. In some boys I have found that the skin does not harden for years.

B   The sweep's house:

C   Another sweep spoke of two of the job's dangers:

I had boys as young as 5½ years, but I did not like them; they were too weak. I was afraid they might go off. They go off just as quietly as you might fall asleep in the chair, by the fire there.

I have known eight or nine sweeps lose their lives by the sooty cancer. The parts which it seizes are entirely eaten off, caused by 'sleeping black' and breathing the soot in all night.

D Many climbing boys were orphans from workhouses because poor feeding had made them skinny. But poor mothers often sold children, especially **illegitimate** ones, for as little as 50p.

E An inquest found that one boy died from 'bad weather':

February 1808: a climbing apprentice of Lambeth was sent at three in the morning to sweep some chimneys at Norwood. The snow was so deep, and the cold so extreme, that a watchman said that he would not have sent even a dog out.

The boy, having swept two chimneys, was returning home with another boy, but found the cold so extreme that he could go no further. He was taken to a public house at Dulwich, and died within an hour.

The master sweep was brought before the magistrate. His main fault appeared to be sending the boy out so early and he was dismissed. An Inquest was held and the verdict was, Died from the Inclemency [harshness] of the Weather.

F A London sweep told Henry Mayhew in the 1840s:

I was a climbing boy and sarved a rigler printiceship for seven years. I niver thought of anythink but climbing: it wasn't so bad at all as some people would make you believe. In narrow flues, such as 23 cm ones, you must slant it; you must have your sides in the angles – it's widest there – and go up that way.

I niver got to say stuck myself, but a many of them did; yes, and were taken out dead. They were smothered for want of air, and the fright, and a stayin' so long in the flue; you see the waistband of their trousers sometimes got turned down in the climbing and, in narrow flues, then they got stuck.

G Two climbing boys killed (1825).

1 Make up a class drama on this topic. The scene is a Committee of Enquiry and five MPs are to hear evidence from master sweeps and climbing boys. Decide what other witnesses you want to call. The Committee want to get at the truth, so the members need to work out their questions in advance. The witnesses need to be equally clear. You can either tape the event or act it to a group of younger pupils.

2 Prepare a class display. You could include:
 * letters to newspapers about it
 * posters to publicise what is happening
Use your library to find out more on the subject.

20 . . . and Match Girls

phosphorus lethal luminous
socialist subscription
'New Model Unions' 'phossy jaw'
'dockers' tanner'

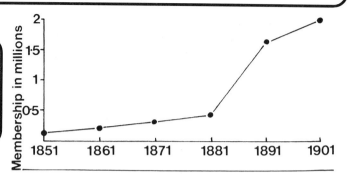
Trade union membership.

The second half of the 19th century saw new attempts to form trade unions to protect workers. These unions were quite different from the Grand National Consolidated of 1834.

The first of these new unions was the Amalgamated Society of Engineers, founded in 1851. It was such a success that other skilled men, such as carpenters, soon copied the idea.

These 'New Model Unions' were a success because their members were skilled workers. They could afford to pay a union **subscription** of 5p a week. This money was used to pay full-time staff, including a Secretary.

They did not expect sudden changes; instead, they worked to improve working conditions for members. But, of course, their members were in demand. Employers needed their skills.

The unskilled workers were in a totally different position. Dock workers, for instance, were lucky to earn even 30p a week, but there was no shortage of them. Organising a union for them was going to be difficult.

Bryant and May's factory in 1871.

Making matchboxes at home for Bryant and May in 1871.

So it was perhaps a surprise that the first successful strike by unskilled workers was by very poorly-paid workers indeed. They were the match girls who produced **phosphorus** matches. Some were made at home under the domestic system; others were made in factories.

The phosphorus was melted and stirred up with glue to make a paste. Then, bundles of matches were dipped in it by hand. Afterwards, they were shaken and dried. It was not difficult work: much of it was done by children. But it was dangerous.

Warm phosphorus smells fishy. Quite early on, it was also found that the fishy fumes were **lethal**. To start with, a worker might get toothache, as the fumes attacked the teeth.

After many months of pain, the teeth rotted and fell out. Some workers walked the streets all night because they could not get to sleep.

However, the disease did not stop with the teeth. It spread to the jaw. Workers called it 'phossy jaw'. Bits of the jawbone rotted away; sometimes, it had to be completely removed. One in eight workers probably caught it; a few of them died.

Often, the conditions in which these people worked increased the dangers. Many factories did not have enough fresh air; workers ate their food off tables dirty with phosphorus; unwashed clothes stank of it. Because it was **luminous**, workers often shone on a dark night.

Striking matchgirls!

In the East End of London, about 1400 girls worked at Bryant and May's match factories. Many had skin diseases because there was nowhere to wash their hands. Some went bald. They all had to put up with heavy fines out of their weekly wages of 20p (girls) or 40p (women).

They were poor and uneducated yet, when they went on strike, they won. It was mainly because a determined **socialist** named Annie Besant helped them. She got them publicity; she found them support and money.

In less than a fortnight, the girls were promised better conditions. The fines were ended and box-fillers were give a nine per cent pay rise. It was a milestone in union history and other victories soon followed. In 1889, the gas workers demanded – and got – an eight-hour day.

Later that year, the London dockers went on strike. Their main demand was for a minimum wage of 2½p an hour. They called it the 'dockers' tanner'. (A 'tanner' was a coin worth 2½p.) It was a long and bitter strike but, in the end, they also won.

Reminder of the dockers' strike, 1889.

1 Each of these dates is important in trade union history. Put them in chronological order and explain what happened in that year:
1889; 1834; 1851.

2 a) Give two reasons why it was hard for unskilled workers to go on strike.
b) Give two reasons why the Engineers' Union was a success.

3 a) Which of the pictures do you think are primary sources?
b) Describe what each of the people is doing in the lower picture on page 74.
c) How would the photograph on this page help the girls?

4 a) If you were Annie Besant, which of these actions would you have taken to get support:
1) Led a march into the West End of London;
2) Got newspapers to print pictures of the girls' working conditions;
3) Got some girls interviewed on television;
4) Organised a petition to take to Parliament;
5) Arranged big public meetings.
Give reasons for the actions you choose.
b) In the library, find out what she *did* do.

councillor   chaperone

In Victorian times, most working women faced a lifetime of hard work and poverty, while middle-class wives had a life of ease, with servants to do the housework. But, in one way, their lives were the same, simply because they were women.

Victorian Britain was controlled by men. All the Members of Parliament were men; only men could vote in elections; men had all the key jobs in society.

Most well-off fathers did not think education was important for their daughters. They believed it was good enough for a girl to be able to sing, dance, play the piano and be good company. Her duty was to get married and her education got her ready for this. Her father's main aim was to train his daughter for marriage and get her off his hands. The last thing he thought of was love.

However, marriage did not bring a woman freedom. Instead of obeying her father, she had to obey her husband. All her money and possessions now belonged to her husband and he could do what he liked with them.

If she had a job and earned money, he could take that, too. Even their children belonged to him. If the parents separated, the children stayed with him.

However, changes were on the way. The years after 1850 saw great changes for both married and single women. Women such as Frances Buss

A A punishment for nagging wives (1812).

opened schools to give girls as good an education as boys had. Meanwhile, women such as Florence Nightingale showed that women could have useful careers.

By 1900, all girls went to school and could sit exams, just as the boys could. They could even go on to university. Many women worked as teachers, shop assistants or in offices, operating one of the new typewriters or telephones.

One major change was that they were allowed to vote in local elections and could become local **councillors**. However, attitudes had not changed completely. They still could not vote in national elections, nor could they become MPs. These were rights which had to wait until our own century.

HOW WOMEN'S RIGHTS INCREASED

1839

IF PARENTS SEPARATED CHILDREN UNDER 7 SHOULD STAY WITH THEIR MOTHER

1857

WIVES COULD DIVORCE HUSBANDS WHO WERE CRUEL OR LEFT THEM

1870

WIVES WERE ALLOWED TO KEEP MONEY THEY EARNED

1891

WIVES COULD NOT BE FORCED TO LIVE WITH HUSBANDS UNLESS THEY WISHED

B   The Countess of Desart gave this advice about why girls should have chaperones in 1897. (Chaperones were older women who accompanied younger ones in public.)

We insist on chaperoning our girls, not because we do not trust them, nor because we do not trust our friends; but because we wish to keep the women-children as long as we may 'unspotted from the world'.

Is a girl improved in any way by having to defend herself from the man she does not care for, from the tricks of the rival she has to look out for? Is it not better for her, and for the husband who may come, that we should do the fighting and the looking-out for her? That we should find the man, and then leave her with her eyes clear to make up her mind and enable him to make up his mind, concerning the future for them both?

C   Some female employment figures, 1901:

1 740 800 domestic servants
124 000 teachers
68 000 nurses
212 female doctors
2 architects

D   Cartoon showing the fight for equal rights (1870):

E   Queen Victoria, writing about women (1870) . . .

Let woman be what God intended, a helpmate for man, but with totally different duties and vocations.

F   . . . and about the burden of child-bearing (1841):

Men seldom think what a hard task it is for us women to go through this *very often*. But God's will be done, and if He decrees that we are to have a great number of children, we must try to bring them up as useful members of society.

G   Joseph Thomson sold his wife in 1832. This was what he told possible buyers:

Gentlemen, I offer my wife, Mary Anne Thomson, whom I mean to sell to the highest bidder. It is her wish as well as mine to part for ever. She has been to me only a born serpent. I took her for my comfort, and the good of my home; but she became my tormentor, a domestic curse and a daily devil.

Now I have told you her faults, I will introduce the bright and sunny side of her. She can read novels and milk cows; she can laugh and weep with the same ease that you could take a glass of ale when thirsty. She can make butter and scold the maid.

She cannot make rum, gin or whisky, but she is a good judge of the quality from long experience in tasting them. I therefore offer her for the sum of 50 shillings [£2.50].
[He sold her after an hour for £1 and a dog.]

1   a) Write down each of these dates on separate lines:
1839;1857;1870;1891.
Beside each, write down what happened then.
b) For *each* event, explain how the law improved the position of women.

2   a) Which of these words do you think describe Victorian men's attitudes towards women:
caring; superior; generous; fair; hostile; unjust; indifferent; inferior? Give reasons.
b) Why do you think they thought like this?

3   a) Read evidence B. What reasons does the writer give for girls having chaperones?
b) Why do you think girls no longer have to be accompanied like this?
c) How would *you* feel if your mother insisted on somebody going with you?

4   a) What most surprises you about evidence G?
b) What reasons would you give Queen Victoria either for agreeing or disagreeing with her?

5   The ducking stool was just for wives. There has never been a similar punishment for men.
Either describe or draw your own punishment for a man who is selfish, lazy or mean. Briefly explain why you think it would work.

22 Schools

nonconformist
Dame Schools   Sunday School
monitor   monitorial system
Revised Code   'payment by results'

In 1800, roughly one child in 20 went to school. They were mostly the sons of rich parents who sent them to public schools or grammar schools. These had changed very little since the 17th century.

Most poor children were too busy working to go to school, although a few schools did exist for them. For instance, there were the Dame Schools. These cost just a few pence a week and, if you were lucky, your child might learn to read and even write. But these ladies were not trained teachers; most were little more than child-minders.

Part-time education was given in factory schools, which became more common after the 1830s. Or there were the Sunday Schools, made popular by Robert Raikes. Sunday School pupils spent most of their time reading the Bible and learning about it. Writing was rare – many of the teachers themselves could not write.

It was the churches which did most to teach the great mass of British children. The Church of England set up the National Society; the **Nonconformist** churches had begun the British & Foreign Schools Society. But money was tight: this had to be education on the cheap.

So they worked out a cheap way to run schools. The master taught the older boys; then, they taught the younger ones. The older children were called monitors so the system was known as the Monitorial system.

It meant that a lot of the work just involved learning things by heart and being able to repeat them. Thinking was less important than remembering. Discipline was harsh; the cane was often used.

It was a start – but Scotland still had much better education than England or Wales; so did most of Europe. As the years passed, the government had to put more and more money into education.

As the cost increased, the government became worried that it might not be getting good value. In 1862, Robert Lowe introduced a plan to make sure that schools were doing their job. His Revised Code arranged for schools to be paid on the basis of how well their pupils did in exams.

The government decided, in 1870, that *all* children would have to go to school. More machines meant that the country needed workers who were better educated; more business meant more letters and accounts. People just had to be able to read, write and do arithmetic.

There were objections to making education compulsory. Some of the upper class said it was dangerous to educate the lower classes. And parents complained because their children could not work and earn money. However, by 1900, every child under 12 went to school.

A What the Bishop of Manchester thought (1861):

We must make up our minds to see the last of the peasant boy at 10 or 11. I think it is quite possible to teach a child all that he needs to know by the time he is 11 years old.

B The monitorial system was devised by Joseph Lancaster and Andrew Bell. This picture shows one of Bell's schools.

C Joseph Lancaster explained his system (1803):

My school is attended by 300 scholars. The WHOLE system of tuition is almost entirely conducted by boys. The school is divided into classes; to each a lad is appointed as monitor. He is responsible for the morals, improvement, good order and cleanness of the class. It is his duty to make reports of progress, [stating] the number of lessons, boys present, absent, etc., etc.

As we expect these boys to leave school when their education is complete, they are instructed to train other lads as assistants who, in future, may [replace] them.

D The sort of problems set to children under 11:

Question 2: What is that number which contains 604, 137 times?
Question 4: Fifty hens laid an egg a day every other day for 28 days. What profit would be made by selling the eggs at 1½p each if the hens cost ½p each day for their food?

1   Match up each name in list A with the correct description from list B:

List A   *List B*
Dame Schools   began payment by results
Sunday Schools   monitors were taught by
                                    teachers and they then taught
                                    younger pupils
grammar schools   taught reading and writing,
                                    based on the Bible
monitorial
schools   taught mainly Greek and Latin
the Revised Code   schools run for poor children

2   a) Look at evidence B. Write down who, or what, you can see at numbers 1 – 3.
b) Look at numbers 4 and 5. What kinds of lesson are going on here?

3   a) Read evidence C. What advantages and disadvantages did this system have?
b) Read evidence A. Do you think this *was* true? Give reasons.
c) Would the Bishop's view be true today? Again, give reasons for your answer.

4   a) Read evidence D. How do these lessons compare with your lessons?
b) Work out the answers to the questions. If you can't do it, copy it out and see if your parents can!

23 Medicine

A An 18th century operation, without anaesthetic.

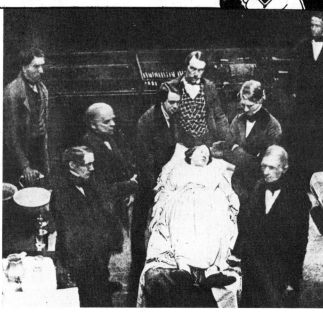

B An operation, using an anaesthetic, in 1847.

> **infection   carbolic**
> ether   anaesthetic   germ   vaccine

Life had improved in many ways by 1900 but perhaps the greatest strides of all were in medicine. For centuries, hospitals had killed more people than they cured. Surgeons had had the skill to save their patients by operating on them. Even so, their patients often still died. Either the sheer pain of the operation or **infection** killed them.

Doctors in the 19th century found the solution. They put their patients to sleep. At first, the drug they used was ether so they talked of 'giving a patient an anaesthetic'. We still do today.

It *was* a great step forward but it did not stop people dying after operations. In fact, there were now more people dying because there were more operations. The reason was that surgeons did not understand the need for cleanliness.

As a result, patients often became infected after an operation. By 1900, this, too, was being solved.

Operating theatres had been made cleaner and doctors were more aware of the need to guard against germs. **Carbolic** sprays were used to stop infection spreading.

On top of that, the hospitals themselves were improving; so was the standard of the nursing. Thanks mainly to Florence Nightingale, there were 64 000 trained nurses.

In 1714, people had been afraid to go into hospital. They looked on it as a death sentence – and an expensive one. By 1900, hospitals had become places where people could – and did – get better.

More lives were being saved outside hospital as well, thanks to the use of vaccines. Killer diseases such as smallpox could now be dealt with by vaccinating the patient. People were also healthier because they were much cleaner. Cheaper soap was on sale and shops stocked cheap cotton clothes, which were easier to keep clean.

However, medical treatment was not cheap – and most people still had to pay to see a doctor or enter hospital. Free treatment for every person in Britain did not come about till the 20th century.

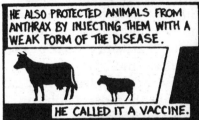

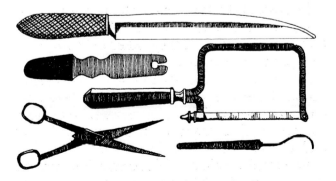

1 Write one sentence to explain each word in the word box.

2 a) Copy out and complete this paragraph:
   Louis _____, a French _____, vaccinated animals to keep them safe from _____. He also claimed that many diseases were caused by tiny creatures called _____. Joseph _____ used _____ solution to keep his patients' wounds clean.

   b) In your own words, explain how Jenner and Simpson helped improve people's health.

3 Look at evidence A and B.
   a) Describe the scene in evidence A.
   b) Do you think this is realistic?
   c) Why does the patient in evidence B stand a better chance of surviving?
   d) What differences are there between B and a modern operation?

4 Look at the picture below of a surgeon's instruments in the 18th century. Write down what you think each instrument was used for.

bank holiday   croquet   music-hall
promenade

In 1800, few people had holidays, except for Sundays and church festivals. Most people worked on Saturday afternoons until 1850, and it was 1871 before Parliament gave people **bank holidays** for the first time.

It was the railways which gave people the chance to make the most of holidays. Trains took people to horse race meetings, which had once been mainly for the rich. And people travelled by train to football matches.

These matches were no longer just rough village events, without rules. Football was becoming quite an industry. The FA Cup had begun in 1871 and, by 1900, players were being paid to play. By then, the goals had crossbars (instead of a tape) and proper nets.

Meanwhile, many old amusements were dying out. The RSPCA had been set up in 1824 and cruel sports which had amused people for centuries at last became illegal. Cock-fighting and bear-baiting were two sports which were banned.

One big change was that it became respectable for ladies to join in sporting events. **Croquet** was popular in the 1860s, but lawn tennis replaced it in the 1870s; hockey became common in the late 1880s, followed by golf after 1890.

A   1882: women playing a new sport.

It was an age of new sports and entertainments, such as the **music-hall**. And, in the middle of the century, people discovered a new source of pleasure which was completely free. It was the seaside.

Bathing in the sea had amused the rich in the 18th century. In Victorian times, railways took poorer people there to join in the fun. Seaside towns, such as Blackpool and Southend, began to attract day-trippers in their thousands.

By 1900, they were not just spending a day there; the middle classes and even some working people were having a week's holiday. Boarding houses were built for them to stay in; piers and **promenades** were built for their amusement. Holidays were here to stay.

NEW SPORTS....NEW RULES....NEW COMPETITIONS

| RUGBY FOOTBALL 1823 | TENNIS INVENTED 1874 | BALLOONING TAKES OFF! | QUEENSBERRY RULES 1866 | COUNTY CHAMPIONSHIP BEGINS, 1873 | 1ST TEST MATCH IN ENGLAND, 1880 | WIMBLEDON 1877 | FOOTBALL LEAGUE 1888 |

How sport developed in the 19th century.

C The scene at the seaside:

Look at these sands! They appear one moving mass of cabs, cars, carts and carriages; horses, ponies, dogs, donkeys, and boys; men, women, children and nurses; and, the least and the biggest – babies and bathing-machines.

Imagine of course all proper accompaniments: little boys with spades; nurses with babies; mammas with sewing; young ladies with novels; young gentlemen with Byron (that is, poems by Byron), canes and eye-glasses; older ones with newspapers, sticks and spectacles.

Then the hawkers are a most noisy, important and persevering [group] here: such opportunities for 'cheap bargains'; nothing in the world that you mayn't buy, from a puppy-dog to 'a yard of cushion-lace, for the low price of one penny farthing' [about ½p]; from a pincushion to a garden chair; from a threepenny doll to a nightcap or a pair of garters.

D The final placings in the first football league table:

	P	W	D	L	Goals For	Goals Against	Points
Preston North End	22	18	4	0	74	15	40
Aston Villa	22	12	5	5	61	43	29
Wolverhampton Wanderers	22	12	4	6	50	37	28
Blackburn Rovers	22	10	6	6	66	45	26
Bolton Wanderers	22	10	2	10	63	59	22
West Bromwich Albion	22	10	2	10	40	46	22
Accrington	22	6	8	8	48	48	20
Everton	22	9	2	11	35	46	20
Burnley	22	7	3	12	42	62	17
Derby County	22	7	2	13	41	60	16
Notts County	22	5	2	15	39	73	12
Stoke	22	4	4	14	26	51	12

B The sands at Ramsgate in 1887. Notice how many clothes people wore even when on the beach.

1 Match up each date with the correct event:
   1871   Football League competition began
   1874   bank holidays introduced
   1880   tennis invented
   1888   the first test match in cricket

2 a) What sport is shown in evidence A?
   b) List all the ways in which this is different to a modern game of this sport.
   c) Why do you think it caught on quickly?

3 a) Look at evidence B and write down what you can see at the numbered places.
   b) How does this scene differ from today?
   c) Which things mentioned in evidence C can you see in evidence B?
   d) Which costumes in evidence B do you find (i) most surprising and (ii) most attractive?

4 Imagine you were spending a day at the seaside in the 19th century and wanted to send a friend a postcard. On a piece of card, write your message; on the other side, draw a seaside scene.

83

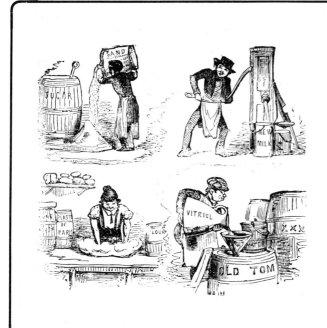

A How food and drink were made! A cartoon of 1845.

B A shop, around 1900.

In 1800, the poor did not spend much time shopping. They did not have the money. In any case, workers were often paid partly in goods or in tokens which had to be spent at the employer's truck shop.

The goods on sale were often overpriced and sometimes of poor quality. But the workers had little choice: either they accepted it or they found another job. Truck shops gradually died out during the 19th century.

Other shops might charge fairer prices, but they were often just as dirty. Nearly everything was sold loose and had to be weighed out and served by the assistant. People were used to finding dead flies in the butter. Even the milk often carried diseases.

In 1844, one group of workers took matters into their own hands. In Rochdale, 28 weavers saved up their money and opened a small shop, selling good quality goods. They also offered a bonus: profits would be shared out among members. They called it a dividend. The more you bought, the bigger your dividend.

The idea was a great success. It was the start of the Co-operative Movement. Today, it still exists, running 'Co-Ops' all around the country.

The second half of the century saw other improvements. The invention of **refrigeration** made it possible to bring meat from Australia. The first frozen lamb arrived in 1880. It also meant fish could be sold further inland. 'Railway milk' began to appear at the same time.

Tinned food became more common during the century. With the use of **pressure-cookers** after 1874, it also became more hygienic. In the following year, the Food and Drugs Act made it possible to check on the quality of food on sale.

At the same time, there were many new shops which were keen to advertise just how pure their food was. These were the new chain stores. In 1869, John Sainsbury opened his first dairy in London; two years later, Thomas Lipton opened his first grocery shop in Glasgow.

These shops bought goods in bulk and sold them cheaply, an idea also used by another new trader called Marks and Spencer. Other famous modern shops, such as Boots, the chemists, and W H Smith, the newsagents, were already becoming a common sight in British high streets. By 1900, Britain was well on the way to the sort of shops we enjoy today.

refrigeration   pressure-cooker
dividend   Co-operative Movement

C   This writer described being paid in truck, 1845:

In nearly two years, all the money I received of my employer was 82½p and 52½p of that I had to pay interest on the pawn-tickets where I had pledged things for necessities for my wife and family.

When Saturday night came, I had to turn out with some meat and candles or tobacco or ale or whatever I had drawn as wages to dispose of at a serious loss. I used to take a can of ale to the barber to get shaved with and a can of ale to the sweep to sweep my chimney. I used to take in a newspaper and I was obliged to take a pound of candles at 3p and leave it for the newspaper which cost 1¾p. I used to take beef at 3p a pound and sell it to the coal woman for 2p.

D   A collier's wife described a truck shop, 1843:

About a month or six weeks ago, I went from home at 11 o'clock; I was there certainly before 12, and it was 8 o'clock at night before I got home, having only called to leave some tommy [truck] goods on the road and was not delayed five minutes.

There was a great crowd to get flour, and when I got it I was forced to stay or else I should not have got anything for my children or my husband. He was hurt in the knee and most of his pay was in goods; 75p was paid out of £1.

When at last I got into the shop my bonnet was off and my apron was all torn, with the women all trying who should get in first. There were two women carried off who had fainted, and I helped them to come to themselves.

And there was a little boy who wanted a loaf of bread for his mother; and having no dinner, he was quite smothered and I thought he was dead and the sweat poured off him. They carried him up to bed, but he went home afterwards.

E   An early Sainsbury's shop:

F   Thomas Lipton explained his success:

Secret of my success? Make no secret. Advertise. That's the secret of it. Advertise all you can. Never miss a chance of advertising.

G   And Jesse Boot explained his success:

There was nothing remarkable about my methods. They were simply common sense. I found that everywhere articles, especially drugs, were being sold at ridiculously high prices, and were sold without any regard to neatness and attractiveness.

My idea was simply to buy tons where others bought hundredweights or less, thus buying more cheaply. And I made all the articles I sold look as attractive as possible. I made, too, a substantial reduction to customers who bought a quantity.

1   Explain each word in the word box.
2   a) Look at evidence A. Write down what each trader is doing in this cartoon.
b) Explain why they are doing this.
3   a) Read evidence C and D. In your own words, explain how the truck system worked.
b) What was wrong or unfair about it?
c) Why was there such shoving in the shop in evidence D?

d) Some wives were in favour of the system. Try to work out why.
4   a) Read evidence F and G. Write down the reasons each person gives for his success.
b) Which do you think is the better reason? Give *your* reasons for your answer.
5   What advantages were there in shopping at Sainsbury's (evidence E) compared with the shop in evidence B?

26   It's a Small World . . .

Before 1840, you paid to *receive* a letter, not to send one.

Britain's Empire was growing throughout the 19th century. So people needed to find better ways of passing news from one part to another. Of course, there were no televisions or radios. For most of the period, the quickest way to send information was by messenger. However, as industry grew, this became too slow and costly.

From 1784 onwards, it was possible to send a letter by mail coach but it was still expensive. The more sheets you used, the more it cost. In any case, the person to whom you were writing had to pay for it. If they refused, your letter was not delivered.

Many people thought it was rather a poor system. One of them was an ex-teacher called Rowland Hill. He argued that the Post Office should charge just 1d (less than ½p) for a letter, no matter how far it was sent. More important, people should pay to *send* a letter, not to receive it.

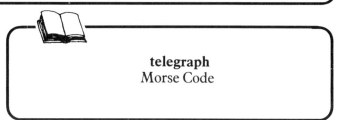

telegraph
Morse Code

So, in 1840, the world's first postage stamp was put on sale – penny postage had arrived. After 1898, Britons could send a letter anywhere in the Empire for just 1d.

The railways had meant that people had to be able to send messages more quickly. It was necessary for railway safety. In 1837, William Cooke and Charles Wheatstone provided a solution when they patented their electric **telegraph**.

The Great Western Railway used the system in 1838, but it was an awkward device. Needles on the instrument had to point out each letter of the message in turn.

There was a better way. By using a code for each letter, the operator could send a message by giving long and short taps on the transmitter. The code was named after its inventor, Samuel Morse. The first successful telegraph cable was laid across the Atlantic Ocean in 1866 and, by 1900, almost the whole world was covered by the system.

Meanwhile, Alexander Graham Bell had come up with an even better idea. In 1876, he sent the first message using *his* new invention – the telephone.

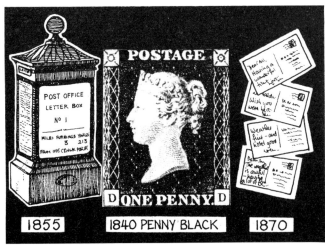

Developments in the postal service.

An early telephone in use.

A *The Times* commented on the telephone, 1879:

The human voice can be conveyed in full force from any one point to any other 8 km off; and with some loss of power, to a very much more considerable distance still.

B Telephone advertisement of 1878:

BELL'S TELEPHONE.

THE ELECTRIC TELEPHONE COMPANY,

115, CANNON STREET, E.C.,

IS NOW READY TO EXECUTE ORDERS

FOR THE

Rental or Purchase of Telephones.

ESTIMATES

ARE ALSO FURNISHED

For the CONSTRUCTION of TELEPHONIC LINES.

Local Companies will be established in all the principal Towns of the United Kingdom.

The public is hereby cautioned against purchasing or using cheap imitations of Bell's Telephone, as they are infringements of Professor Bell's Patent. All makers, sellers, or users of such spurious instruments will be prosecuted to the full extent of the law.

C Better postal services encouraged people to send greetings cards. This is a Victorian valentine card.

A	•—	J	•———	S	•••
B	—•••	K	—•—	T	—
C	—•—•	L	•—••	U	••—
D	—••	M	——	V	•••—
E	•	N	—•	W	•——
F	••—•	O	———	X	—••—
G	——•	P	•——•	Y	—•——
H	••••	Q	——•—	Z	——••
I	••	R	•—•		

D The Morse Code is still in use.

1 a) Unjumble these letters to find the names of five inventors:
    (i) SMOUL REASEM (ii) HOWARD N LILL (iii) MICKIE WALLOO
    (iv) SETH ART ACHOSE WELN
    (v) GRANDEER XALL BALEHAM.
   b) Write down each name and what he invented.

2 a) This message is in Morse Code. What does it say?
   b) Write the answer – in code, of course!

   •— — ••• —— —— •• —• ••—• • —• — • — ••— —— —•

3 a) Write down all the advantages of having (i) postage stamps and (ii) telephones.
   b) Are there any disadvantages?

4 a) The 1d Black stamp was the world's first postage stamp. How is it different from a modern British stamp?
   b) Imagine you had the job of designing the first stamp. The only restriction is that you must include the Queen's head and the price. Design your own 1d stamp.

5 In the early days, the distress signal in Morse Code was CQD. Now, SOS is used instead. Look at evidence D. Why do you think it was changed to SOS?

How ships changed during the 19th century.

There was another reason why the world seemed a smaller place by 1900. Transport had got even faster. In the 18th century, people sailed the seas in sailing ships made of wood. By 1900, they used ships built of steel and powered by steam.

James Watt's steam engine was much too big to use successfully on a ship, and it used up too much coal. A small, high-pressure boiler was needed before ships could use steam power.

In 1802, William Symington launched his second steamship, the *Charlotte Dundas*, on the Forth and Clyde Canal. It towed two barges for 30 km. Ten years later, Henry Bell's *Comet* began a regular service on the River Clyde. And, in 1819, the *Savannah* crossed the Atlantic, using steam power for part of the journey. It took 27 days.

But these early steamships used **paddle-wheels**. The real future for steamships lay in having a **propeller** fitted. The first propeller-driven ship to cross the Atlantic was the *Great Britain*, designed by Brunel. It took just 14 days in 1845.

| paddle-wheels | propeller |
| Red Flag Act | airship |

However, by the end of the century, it was a new form of land transport which was taking people's fancy. For years, people had been trying to make a successful 'horseless' carriage.

In 1769, a Frenchman, Nicholas Cugnot, had built the first steam carriage. It managed a speed of 3½ km an hour, which was actually slower than walking! Anyway, it knocked down a wall on an early run. Cugnot was put in prison.

Later inventors were not so unlucky. Karl Benz, a German, made the first successful petrol-driven vehicle in 1885. It could reach 16 km an hour, although the police tried to stop it doing so!

Benz's cars were soon on sale for about £140 each and, in 1891, he began producing four-wheel cars. Another early manufacturer was Gottlieb Daimler. He and Benz are often called the 'fathers of the motor car'.

However, no car was seen in Britain until 1895 because the Red Flag Act kept the speed limit down to 6½ km per hour. It was just too slow for motor cars.

The red flag was no longer needed by 1895, although a man still had to walk in front.

An early Benz car, 1888.

Parliament was persuaded to abolish the Act in the following year and the speed limit went up to 19 km per hour. Motorists celebrated by holding a special trip from London to Brighton in which 33 cars took part. A piece of red cloth was torn up before they set off.

However, some people were far from keen on this new form of transport. Queen Victoria did not find cars amusing. She thought they 'smell exceedingly nasty and are very shaky and disagreeable'.

But she was an old lady. She had been born over 60 years before the motor car. When it first appeared in Britain, her reign was nearly at an end. So was the 19th century.

She could be forgiven for not guessing that the motor-car would revolutionise life in our century, as the railway had in hers.

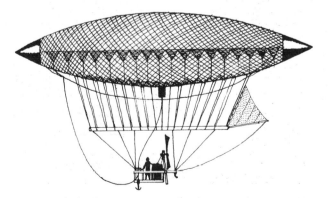

Man was beginning to conquer the air, too. By 1900, airships were using petrol motors and had aluminium frames.

A A car journey in the 1890s:

Motoring was an adventure. I remember staying at a country house some 16 kilometres from the nearest station, whose owner had one of those new-fangled spit-fires.

At the end of our stay, a cart with our luggage started [for the station] an hour and a half before the time of the train. Twenty minutes later, the motor set off with those who were daring enough to trust themselves to it. A quarter of an hour after the motor, a brake with a pair of fast horses [left] so that, if the motor had broken down, it would pick up [its passengers] and convey them to the station.

On this occasion the motor behaved surprisingly well. In spite of having to stop whenever a horse-drawn vehicle appeared, while the terrified animal was led past it, it came within sight of the luggage-cart 800 metres from the station. It arrived there a quarter of an hour before the brake. So those great strong horses had not gained on us after all!

1 Answer these questions in full sentences:
a) Why was steel a better material for building ships than wood?
b) What part did these men play in developing steamships: (i) Symington; (ii) Bell?
c) What was special about the Atlantic crossing by the *Great Britain*?
d) What did Nicholas Cugnot invent?
e) What was Karl Benz's major achievement?

2 a) Explain in your own words why the Red Flag Act made driving in Britain difficult.
b) Suppose you were a car-driver in 1896 and wanted Parliament to end the Red Flag Act. Write a letter to your local paper, giving good reasons why the Act is a nuisance.

3 a) Which of the pictures on these two pages is evidence? Explain how you decided.
b) Read evidence A. Which things mentioned would not be part of a modern car journey?

4 a) List the differences in our lives today if there were no motor-cars.
b) Choose what you think is the biggest difference and give reasons for your choice.

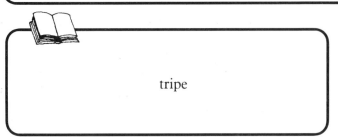

tripe

At midnight on December 31st 1900, people all over the world were staying up to welcome the 20th century. In one dance-hall, the guests dropped messages into a huge iron box. It was sealed up and will be opened again in the year 2000.

What were those messages about, one wonders? Almost certainly, they were messages of hope. The 19th century had seen such great changes and most of them had been for the better.

Perhaps the most obvious changes had been at home. The middle-class family of 1900 had baths with hot and cold water; the rooms were lit by gas; coal fires kept them warm in high rooms with wallpaper on the walls and carpets on the floor.

A The first Kodak camera appeared in 1888. It used a roll of film, which made it easier to carry around. It took round photographs.

A VICTORIAN KITCHEN

WASHING MACHINE AND MANGLE

COAL-FIRED COOKING RANGE

A NEW GAS COOKER

KNIFE CLEANER

FRESH MEAT FROM AUSTRALIA

SCULLERY

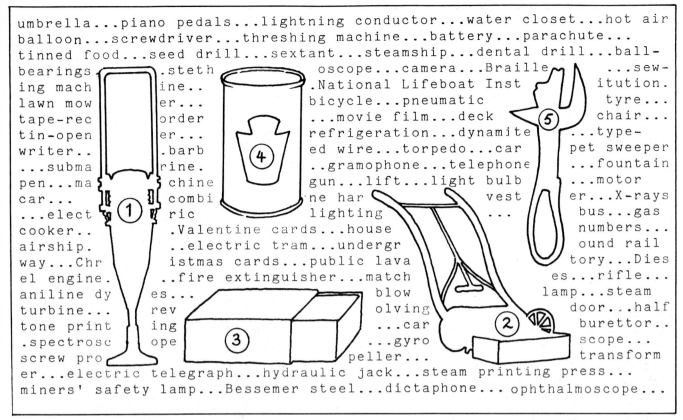

```
umbrella...piano pedals...lightning conductor...water closet...hot air
balloon...screwdriver...threshing machine...battery...parachute...
tinned food...seed drill...sextant...steamship...dental drill...ball-
bearings         .steth         oscope...camera...Braille     ...sew-
ing mach         ine..         .National Lifeboat Inst         itution.
lawn mow         er...         bicycle...pneumatic              tyre...
tape-rec         order         ...movie film...deck             chair...
tin-open         er...         refrigeration...dynamite         ...type-
writer..         .barb         ed wire...torpedo...car          pet sweeper
...subma         rine.         ..gramophone...telephone         ...fountain
pen...ma         chine         gun...lift...light bulb          ...motor
car...           combi         ne har         vest             er...X-rays
...elect         ric           lighting              ...        bus...gas
cooker..         .Valentine cards...house                       numbers...
airship.         ..electric tram...undergr                      ound rail
way...Chr        istmas cards...public lava                     tory...Dies
el engine.       ..fire extinguisher...match                    es...rifle...
aniline dy    es...                            blow             lamp...steam
turbine...    rev                              olving           door...half
tone print    ing                              ...car           burettor..
.spectrosc    ope                              ...gyro          scope...
screw pro                               peller...               transform
er...electric telegraph...hydraulic jack...steam printing press...
miners' safety lamp...Bessemer steel...dictaphone... ophthalmoscope...
```

Inventions of 1714 to 1900. Many of them have been typed on a typewriter, another 19th-century invention.

For dinner, they might be eating meat brought from Australia and cooked on one of the new gas cookers. They probably lit it with the sort of match we still use.

After their evening meal, they may have read a novel or the daily newspaper. Their children could also read. So could poor children, now that education was free.

At work, too, there had been big improvements. Wages were still rising and people were mostly better off. Most workshops and factories now had strict safety rules. Working hours of women and young people were limited and there were trade unions to look after workers' interests.

Nevertheless, there were still many people who lived in slum houses, without enough to eat. One man reckoned 25 per cent of the people of York were not earning enough to satisfy their basic needs.

More of these people now had the vote and many of them supported the new Labour Party. Its policies attracted the working class and it already had two MPs.

The changes did not end there. The great popular entertainment in Victorian times was the music-hall. Moving pictures would soon replace it. The first public film show in Britain was in 1896.

Before the railways brought fresh fish to inland towns, this was the popular cheap supper: trotters and tripe (animal's stomach), with vinegar. On the right: Britain in 1900.

👤👤👤👤👤👤👤👤👤👤	70% OF THE POPULATION LIVED IN TOWNS OR CITIES
👤👤👤👤	1 IN 4 WORKERS WAS FEMALE
👤46 👤50	AVERAGE AGES OF DEATH
👤👤👤👤👤👤👤👤👤👤	14% OF CHILDREN DIED BEFORE THEY WERE ONE YEAR OLD
●○○○○○○	TRADE UNION MEMBERSHIP: 1 IN 7 OF EMPLOYED MEN. 1 IN 33 OF EMPLOYED WOMEN
■□□□□	BRITAIN PRODUCED ⅓ OF ALL THE WORLD'S MANUFACTURED GOODS
◆→724	1 POLICEMAN TO EVERY 724 PEOPLE
1800 1900	PEOPLE USE FOUR TIMES AS MUCH SOAP AS IN 1800

So people expected great things of the new century. The British probably thought they had more reason to be hopeful than anyone else. True, the United States was now making more goods than Britain, but Britain was still doing more trade than any other country on earth. It had more merchant ships, too.

And it had a bigger navy, which had not been seriously challenged for nearly a century. Of course, it was busy. It had to protect not only Britain but also the British Empire. A quarter of the world's population lived in the Empire. No wonder people felt secure and confident about the future.

The leader of Britain and its great Empire was a frail old lady of 81. She had been queen since 1837. But, in the early days of 1901, her health was declining. As she lay ill at Osborne House on the Isle of Wight, people came to pay their respects.

HE SAYS IT'S THE FIRST PASSENGER AEROPLANE!

One visitor was her grandson, Kaiser William II of Germany. He was also present at her funeral soon afterwards; his behaviour impressed people. One popular paper said that he had found a place in British hearts.

Less than 14 years later, Britain and Germany were fighting each other. The great hopes for the new century died quickly in the trenches of the First World War.

B What some papers said in 1900:

1 Seeing what has been done for women during the last twenty or thirty years, we may well venture to hope still more from the brand-new century.

2 Railway engineers talk of a 100 miles an hour (160 kph) express as one of the triumphs which may be expected in the twentieth century.

3 Two subjects are bound to be uppermost in the programme of social reform that the new century will be called upon to consider. One is the housing of the working classes, and the other pure food.

4 The coming century will be marked by the development by the European powers of vast areas of country beyond the seas. Rightly or wrongly, all the European powers have come to believe that a nation in order to be great must have an oversea Empire.

5 It is an imperfect world, and the 20th century will probably get no nearer to setting it right than the 19th.

1 On the left are items on sale in 1900. Match each one with the object on the right which was used instead of it in 1800.

gas lighting	fire or stove
gas cooker	tinderbox
sewing machine	candles or firelight
tinned food	needle and thread
fountain pen	salted meat and fish
matches	quill

2 Look at the top picture on page 91.
a) Pick out a few inventions which you think made the greatest changes. Give reasons.
b) Look at the five outlines. Write down what you think these objects are.

3 Suppose you had been in the dance-hall on December 31st 1900. Write down your message for people in the future.

4 Look around your classroom. Write down any ten objects which could not have been there in 1900. For each one, explain why it could not have been there.

5 When Marks and Spencer opened their first stall in Leeds market, every item on sale cost 1d (0.4p). Today, you cannot buy anything costing less than 1p. Make a class collection of objects costing 1p. How many can you find?

Revision

1 Crossword. All the answers you need are in this book.

Clues: Across
1. A land agent who campaigned for a ten-hour day. (7)
4. The Tolpuddle labourers were _____ sentenced to transportation. (4)
7. A crime against king or country. (7)
9. His ideas led to a better postal service. (4)
10. Disease was the main reason why a slave might _____ on board ship. (3)
11. What the first postage stamp cost. (5)
12. What a turnpike trust built. (4)
13. A horse-drawn one might have taken you to the Great Exhibition. (3)
16. If you were poor, you might make this with grated toast. (3)
17. At first, third class railway passengers were often *not* this! (3)
18. The match girls' one was a success. (6)
19. He made Coalbrookdale famous. (5)
24. Hot or cold, the middle classes had at least one indoors. (3)
25. Iron _____ comes from the ground. (3)
26. He or she was in prison for owing money. (6)

Clues: Down
1. The Tolpuddle men made a secret one. (4)
2. Climbing boys were assistants to them. (6)
3. After pay day, navvies often went on one. (5)
4. The first anaesthetic. (5)
5. The first bank _____ was in 1871. (7)
8. One of the few things a middle-class girl was taught to do. (4)
13. She led the match girls. (6)
14. The Metropolitan Police had their office next to Scotland _____. (4)
15. An animal or a kind of iron. (3)
16. There was a campaign to limit working hours to this number. (3)
17. Tolpuddle is in this county. (6)
20. In 1714, a constable served for this length of time. (4)
21. People were afraid that a policeman might really be this. (3)
22. Street of the Runners! (3)
23. Mr Ludd. (3)

2 In the picture below, the artist has drawn a street scene in 1900. However, if you look closely, you will see he has included some details which would not have been there in that year. Each time you find one, write it down and explain why it is wrong.

The sheer number of different authors used in this volume makes it difficult to comment usefully on more than a small selection of them. The following sources have been selected as those particularly needing comment.

A Memoir of Robert Blincoe was first published in 1828 and has a rather unusual history. Its author, John Brown, began writing it in 1822 but committed suicide in 1825. Its first publication was without Blincoe's knowledge.

It is often quoted as an example of what conditions were like in the worst mills, especially for apprentices. However, its value to factory reformers was soon realised, as is shown by the title-page of the 1832 edition (below).

The entire text is available in a 1977 reprint by Caliban Books.

A

MEMOIR

OF

ROBERT BLINCOE,

An Orphan Boy;

SENT FROM THE WORKHOUSE OF ST. PANCRAS, LONDON,

AT SEVEN YEARS OF AGE,

TO ENDURE THE

Horrors of a Cotton-Mill,

THROUGH HIS INFANCY AND YOUTH,

WITH A MINUTE DETAIL OF HIS SUFFERINGS,

BEING

THE FIRST MEMOIR OF THE KIND PUBLISHED.

BY JOHN BROWN.

MANCHESTER:

PRINTED FOR AND PUBLISHED BY J. DOHERTY, 37, WITHY-GROVE.

1832.

Care also needs to be taken when considering evidence given to the government enquiry of 1831–2. Witnesses were not questioned on oath and some refused to repeat their statements in 1833. Even Engels, who himself had a somewhat romantic idea of the domestic system, thought that some of the evidence was wrong.

One official who re-examined some of the witnesses in 1833, wrote, 'They have sometimes appeared astonished at the statements reported to have been made by them before the Committee.' Some witnesses denied they had intended to make statements attributed to them the previous year.

In any case, much of the evidence related to conditions which were supposed to have existed many years earlier. Later reports often stressed that accusations of cruelty and suffering were not, in general, true of factories. Also, there were many who believed that conditions in most factories were better than in most workers' own homes.

The Mines Report of 1842 had a greater effect than government reports normally did because of the decision to include pictures. Woodcuts of women and children in the mines, such as that of the girl miner shown above, helped to stir up widespread support for banning child and female labour in the pits.

They also angered mine-owners, such as Lord Londonderry, who told the House of Lords that these pictures 'of an extravagant and disgusting, and in some cases of a scandalous and obscene character' should not 'have been adopted in a grave publication'.

Glossary

apprentice – a person learning a craft or trade
aqueduct – a bridge carrying a water channel
arson – the crime of setting fire to property
attic – a space below the roof in a house

bank holiday – a public holiday
bellows – an instrument used to produce strong air current
blunderbuss – a short gun with a wide muzzle

cab – a horse-drawn carriage for hire
capital crime – a crime for which the criminal can be put to death
carbolic – an acid used for killing germs
carcase – a dead body of an animal
cemetery – a graveyard
charcoal – a black substance made by partly burning wood
civil servant – an official who works for the country
cogs – series of teeth on the edge of a wheel
colliery – a coal-mine
commissioner – an official with a particular job to do
compensation – something given to make up for something else
compulsory – something which you cannot choose not to do
councillor – a member of a council
croquet – a lawn game played by knocking balls through arches

dungheap – a heap of refuse and manure
dysentery – a disease causing diarrhoea

empire – a number of countries ruled by just one government
engineer – a person who plans and builds machines, roads, etc.
excrement – the waste matter discharged from a body

forgeries – not genuine; fakes
friendly society – a society which helps members in need
furnace – a place for making a hot fire to melt iron

gauge – the distance between the rails of a railway
governess – a woman who teaches or looks after children in their own home
gradient – the angle (or steepness) of a slope

heiress – a lady who has been left a lot of money
highwayman – a man who robs road travellers
husbandry – farming

illegitimate – a child whose parents are not married
imported – brought in from a foreign country
infection – a disease caused by germs
initiation ceremony – a special event at which a new member is welcomed into a group
international – involving more than one country
invested – put money into a company to make a profit

lethal – deadly
ley – mixture
licensed – given permission to do something
loom – a machine for weaving cloth
luminous – shining in the dark

magistrate – a local official who acts as a judge
marling – adding lime and clay
memorial – something to remind people of a person or event
middle class – in effect, people who are not working class but earn a living, e.g. doctors, businessmen, shopkeepers
music-hall – a concert-hall for variety shows

National Anthem – 'God Save the Queen' (or King)
navigator – a worker who built a canal or railway
nonconformist – any Protestant *not* in the Church of England

paddle-wheel – a wheel with paddles on it to propel a ship
parish – an area with its own church
patented – registered an invention so that no one else can copy it without paying money to the inventor
pauper – a very poor person who cannot support him/herself
perishable foods – food which can go off and rot
petition – a request, signed by many people
phosphorus – an element which looks like yellow wax
poaching – illegally going on to another person's land to hunt or fish
polluted – made dirty
poor relief – help for the poor, paid for out of taxes
population – the number of people in a certain place
pressure-cooker – a vessel in which heated steam under pressure is used to cook or sterilise
promenade – a place to walk for pleasure
propeller – something with blades on it which, as it goes round, propels a boat (or aeroplane)

refrigeration – a way of keeping something cold
Royal Commission – a group of people chosen by the king or queen to study, and report on, a topic

sewage – the waste matter which goes through a sewer
sewer – a drain to carry away refuse and human **excrement**
shanty town – a group of crudely-built huts
shearing machine – a machine to cut off the nap (rough surface) of woollen cloth
slave – a person owned by another person
slum – a dirty, overcrowded building or area
socialist – a person who believes that a community's interests are more important than those of any individual
soot – black deposit caused by burning coal or wood
spindle – a rod which holds the thread in spinning
subscription – money; fee paid to join something

telegraph – a way of sending messages by electricity
terrace – a row of houses joined together
textile – woven cloth
threshing machine – a machine to separate the grain from corn
tow – a coarse rope
trade union – an organisation of workers to protect their interests
treason – a crime against the king, queen or country
truck shop – a company shop; under the truck system, wages were often given in goods or tokens, not cash

workhouse – a building where poor people had to live and work, if they were able-bodied

Index